To my
Bonnie....

WAC Major: Herstory

Thank you for your
support and inspiration
during these years. It
is so great to have you
as a friend.
Take care and enjoy
yourself and your
grandchildren.
Thanks again...
Luv— "Lenora"

WAC Major: Herstory

A Black Woman in the White Man's Army

VISIT MY WAC MAJOR BOOK BLOG AT:

http://tweety1216.typepad.com/lenora

PLEASE SEND ME YOUR BOOK REVIEW AT:

Lenora1216@aol.com

H. LENORA BYRD

Library of Congress Control Number:		2007900555
ISBN:	Hardcover	978-1-4257-4060-3
	Softcover	978-1-4257-4059-7

This book was printed in the United States of America.

To order additional copies of this book, contact:
Xlibris Corporation
1-888-795-4274
www.Xlibris.com
Orders@Xlibris.com
36994

CONTENTS

Dedication

To my mother, Eunice Byrd, for her love, support, and sacrifices which enabled me to be successful in more ways than one. I am eternally grateful for her example as a single parent, who always encouraged me to *be all that I could be.* I love you, Mom.

To my daughter, Chantay, who is also my best friend, I dedicate this book and my life to you. You were the most precious reward I received during my military journey. Your unconditional love and support, then and now, helped to make me the person I am today. I love you dearly.

To my dear guardian angels: Brigadier General Sherian Cadoria, Major General Jerry Curry, and Colonel Dorothy Spencer. Each of you came to my rescue during times when *the white man* created unnecessary valleys for me to overcome during my military career.

And to my Brownsville high school classmates and other close friends, your inspiration, enthusiasm, and support are second to none. Thank you for giving me the *spark* that has resulted in the publication of this book.

PREFACE

This is not a story about a person who reached the maximum heights of the military-rank structure. Instead, this book relates life at a glance of an unknown black female, army-noncommissioned officer and commissioned officer, who served her country honorably for over twenty years. This book is an intimate portrait about an African-American woman who

- refused to conform to societal traditional roles and opted to serve in an environment that indicated there was no place for a woman in the armed forces;
- served as a *token* during the integration of the Women's Army Corps (WAC) into the all-man army by proving to men that women could shoot pistols, rifles, and shotguns; roll in the dirt and survive field training; read maps, dig a foxhole, endure road marches, do push-ups, sit-ups; and run two or more miles;
- was *born too soon* to reap the opportunities and equality that women now experience in the military;
- and is now a retired, disabled veteran with a small pension, a sixty-six-year-old drawing Social Security, who wonders if her military duty and honor to her country was all worth so much of her life to an organization that caters mainly to and applauds the high white male rollers in the military.

As an adolescent, I never envisioned traveling on a rocky road called life, which would lead me through multifarious valleys. Each obstacle that fell into my path ultimately taught me many valuable lessons for personal awareness and spiritual growth. My youthful dreams turned into a spiritual odyssey with numerous sequels containing adult nightmares that promised me a life of prolonged struggle. I must be destined for strife based on my birth, my birthplace, my family, my sex, my race, my gender preference, and my economical background.

The United States of America is the declared land of the free and the designated home of the brave, which professes that all men are created equal. It is the alleged Promised Land *of the people and for the people,* where all dreams purportedly come true. Somehow, this perspective changed drastically as I traveled and stumbled through this so-called Promised Land. My military experiences and journey revealed

- a bewildering place that forced me to lock horns against constant inequities, rather than sensing a world that granted me an inherent freedom;
- a contradictory land that minimized my courage and bravery, despite my service to my country;
- a land of broken promises where men are indeed equal, but women and people of color are not;
- a flourishing Promised Land *of some* of the people, and only *for certain* people, everlasting dependent upon race, sex, and religion;
- and a paradoxical place where bad things happen to good people for no reason, resulting in random meaninglessness in life.

This so-called Promised Land can force the American dreamer to become cynical, join the bad folks club, or simply give up. My past military career was hurting my present life, so I decided to put my journal notations into book form. Reflection of one's past can be a worthwhile therapeutic tool that can provide clarity and understanding. As I began to write my book, flashbacks of my struggling military journey, coupled with the victories and the lessons learned, came crashing to the forefront of my mind. I felt a pit in my stomach as I asked myself, "Was my life in the army a failure or a success?"

A spiritual voice within kept haunting me with its message: "Don't dwell on the errors and weaknesses in your performance as a soldier, daughter, mother, wife, lover, friend, or associate. You did your very best. Complete each segment of your story, stop looking back, glance forward, and awaken that precious dream lurking within. Free the shackles that bind your radiant inner spirit, learn from your worldly army experience, and always trust in God's guidance. Your past is over—gone, never to be again. Tell your story, end it, and then move briskly forward in search for greater fulfillment and meaning in your life."

As I continued to grapple with writing this book, I kept having misgivings as to whether my story was worth telling. I took writing correspondence courses, subscribed to writers' magazines, researched writing styles and strategies, and read numerous nonfiction books. After reading Colin Powell's autobiography, my enthusiasm dropped to a mournful low. Doubtful thoughts and questions flashed through my head. "Colin Powell, I'm not! Who is going to take the time to read what an 'unknown low-ranking soldier girl' wrote? Who really cares about the army experiences of a black female in the white man's army, compared to the positive climb to the White House by a famous black male, four-star general?"

My continuous doubts and the various lessons that I learned from my writing courses kept throbbing in my mind, haunting me: "Does my story depict the struggles and lives of other people? Is there a shared basis of experience between the readers and me? Are my concerns their concerns? Are my episodes significant enough to give them meaning by shaping them into a story? Who really wants to read about the lessons learned that assisted me in personal awareness, development, and spiritual growth? Do I really want to go through with this?"

"Every life has a story and your life matters!" This message became the final retort for all my doubts and questions. The reflective thoughts, the spiritual messages from within, and the feedback and encouragement from relatives, friends, associates, and instructors compelled me to stick with it and complete my intimate portrait. What would my story do for the reader? We tend to constantly reflect on *who we used to be, how we got here from there, who we are now, and where we are headed tomorrow.* Hopefully, my story will offer insight, inspiration, and spiritual nourishment to readers who feel lost in *their Promised Land* and wondering if his/her life has true meaning. Yes, my story has a message for all.

There comes a time when we frantically attempt to find meaning, intent, and purpose of our past, present, and future lives. We create our own experiences through our hopes and dreams, our beliefs and perceptions, and how we choose to interpret the world and the people in it. When we experience crises and disappointments, we tell ourselves that fulfillment and rewards cannot be far away. A point comes in our lifetime when we stop believing in mankind and put our faith and trust in a higher being. That same higher being tells us that we need only to look within our spiritual souls to find the greatness of human potential. "Every life has a story! As a bird must sing, I must tell my story."

INTRODUCTION

Who am I? I was born into this world an extrovert with an optimistic, mind-set and intense curiosity viewing life through rose-colored glasses. As a child, my environment was generally secure and stable—I was poor and black but raised to be a healthy, happy-go-lucky person. From my earliest recollection, I felt accepted, loved, supported, encouraged, and reassured by my mother; therefore, my self-image as a child was positive. My mother gave birth to me out of wedlock while she was a senior in high school. She always tells me that I was pre-educated in her womb. I don't have any siblings and was raised without a father. Oops, I had no choice but to be an offspring from a dysfunctional family!

What are my personality traits? As a child and adolescent, I had a high energy level, looked on the bright side of life, and welcomed new experiences. I was never a follower, did not need to belong to groups, and was very independent and self-sufficient. My intellectual curiosity developed quickly, and I was somewhat of a daredevil. Fearless in sports and music, causal, and carefree, I spent a good deal more time with boys than with girls. Given my own set of keys and a code of behavior, I always try to honor my mother's trust and do her proud. I guess you could say that I am a typical Sagittarius with the following traits: free-spirited, jovial, trustworthy, expansive, giving, charismatic, genuine, sincere, adaptable, versatile, scholarly, exploratory, inspirational, philosophic, and spiritual. The army taught me to be disciplined, organized, attentive to detail, self-confident, assertive, and to accept the cards dealt to me but to try to play them to win the game. If provoked, I can be candid, outspoken, blunt, intolerant, impulsive, nonconforming, capricious, stubborn, wisecracking, sarcastic, arrogant, subtle, or ambivalent. I seldom meet the expectations of others—I am an individual with a unique personality seeking the *spice of life* that leads to an enjoyable and meaningful destiny. During my military career and to this day, I follow my own path, doing what I desire to do rather than what others want me to do.

What are my physical traits? As a child, I was of average weight and size with blond-colored pigtails—my natural hair color is light auburn, and the sun would turn it so light that I looked like a black Swedish child. I have always been a tomboy, athletic, and conscientious about my looks—copper tone skin with Cherokee Indian bloodline.

I guess at age seven, I was destined to be in the military. Throughout adolescence and adulthood, I maintained my proper weight, walked proudly and tall with a thirty-inch step, and seemed to be "energy in motion" at all times. The army influenced me to cut my hair to shoulder length so it would not touch my collar, and to this day, I wear my hair short and tapered in a very neat cut. At age sixty-six, I am still slim and trim and do not look or act my age.

My mother was dirt-poor and struggled to support us on welfare in an economically deprived coal-mining town in southwestern Pennsylvania. We lived in coal-mining houses with four rooms at the most, complemented with a leaning, rickety outhouse in the backyard. I have this ungodly scar on my right leg from slashing it open when I fell on the sidewalk ice on my way to the bathroom. Never got stitches—Mom couldn't afford it. We heated our bathwater on a coal stove, poured it into a portable oblong tub, and squeezed our naked bodies inside like a clam in an oyster. In the winter months, I bathed near a hot big black Warm Morning stove to keep my body from turning to ice. I still have a distinctive burn scar on my rear end from getting too close to that potbellied stove. Yes, I have my share of childhood scars.

Mom spent the majority of her youth being a caregiver as she nurtured me, my grandmother, and a nephew. Then she took on the task of raising my daughter while I became the breadwinner by serving in the army. She never married; and at age eighty-seven with the dreadful Alzheimer's disease, it astounds me when I realize how long she lived alone. When she was eighty, I asked her what she would do differently in her life; she responded with staid calmness.

"I like my life the way it is, and the way I did things. I wouldn't change my life for anything in the world."

Mom took me everywhere she went, and I followed in her footsteps as she participated in softball games throughout the Pennsylvania valley. This led me to my interest in softball and my dreams of becoming an athlete. At age thirteen, I was the only girl on the boys' baseball team, and I couldn't understand why there weren't any sports for girls. "Get real, child." In 1954, girls were supposed to be feminine rather than tomboy. There weren't any athletic opportunities for me in high school or college during that era—I was a *female, born too soon.*

My father never acknowledged the role he played in my birth, yet I am the spitting image of one of his sisters. It was not until I was forty-two when I decided to track down my father in Chicago. His sister told me where he lived and gave me his address. Ironically, he was a retired army sergeant major, and I wrote him a long letter and enclosed a picture of my daughter and myself. He sent me a signed card with a picture of him taken with President Carter and the governor of Chicago. I guess he was trying to impress me. Not once did he admit to being my father or indicate any concern for me as a person. Eventually, I said "to hell with it" and dismissed this man from my mind and continued with my life. That was twenty some years ago, and he went to his grave without ever acknowledging that I was his daughter.

I had fun as an adolescent and started maturing faster than my peers. When I was fourteen, my mother bought me a guitar for Christmas, and I began teaching myself to play it by listening to the radio. I told myself then that "I'm gonna be a girl athlete as well as a girl musician." My next-door neighbor, a coal miner, who played the guitar, helped me get started on my way. Benny was my best friend's father, and he loved to strum his guitar, playing rhythm and blues. I would watch his long fingers manipulate the strings on his guitar, and I could feel the flow of the music in my veins.

"Lenora, I'm gonna teach you how to play the bass so we can play music together," Benny said with a reassuring grin.

"Okay. Four strings should be easier to play than six strings. Let's do it."

Within months, I learned how to play a bass guitar and sang my lungs out with my deep, velvety contralto voice. I had to learn music the hard way—playing by ear because Mom was too poor to pay for music lessons. To this day, I regret that I didn't take music lessons, especially the piano and guitar. When I turned sixteen, I was ready for the big-time music scene. Benny found us a job with other coal miners, who played the piano and drums and were performing throughout the area. I was an aspiring young singer and bassist, closely chaperoned by these coal miners. Each weekend we traveled down the Monongahela Valley or West Virginia mountains playing rhythm and blues in nightclubs and hotels. After an evening of entertaining, I would drag myself into my house in the wee hours of the morning, loaded down with bass and amplifier, and proudly give my mother my earnings for a one-night performance—$20.

At seventeen, I received personal recognition and satisfaction through my exhibition in sports and music. I was tagged with the nickname "Mama Loochie," which was a hit song of the '50s, and I used to sing it forcefully during our performances. I'm still referred to by this name back home. My army buddies tagged me with the nickname "Lee," short for my middle name Lenora.

Life for me was good as a teenager. I was a member of my biology and French clubs, made the honor roll, attended my Baptist church every Sunday, taught Sunday school, and was enjoying life to the utmost, playing softball and music. My youthful dreams for continued acceleration in education, athletics, and music were a sparkling vision. Then high school graduation came in 1958, and it was time to face the real world. I loved school, but Mom was too poor to send me to college. Suddenly, I felt depressed and downtrodden. I studied and worked hard during my adolescent years, was well-liked, gregarious, and displayed unlimited potential. My dreams of playing softball and music for the rest of my life would not put bread on our table or lead me to a stable career. "Well, Ms. Mama Loochie, let's get with it and find a job."

I feverishly checked the local classified ads, but nothing was available in my hometown in Brownsville. The only alternative was to find a job in Pittsburgh, sixty miles away. I searched and searched, but no one wanted to hire a young eighteen-year-old black girl in a job that would help her to flourish and grow. However, don't despair, because Ms. Lee lucked up and snagged a job as a live-in housekeeper for a Jewish family in Pittsburgh.

I wanted something more rewarding and meaningful, and a little voice whispered to me gently: "Be thankful you have a job, girl. These are hard times, especially for black folk; and it's common for y'all to do housework. After all, black women were born into this Promised Land to be subservient." As I cleaned dirty bathrooms, bedrooms, and did other menial housework duties, the unadorned truth sunk into my naive young soul and ruffled my childhood fantasies. My ego and self-concept dropped fifty notches, but I had no other choice but to grin and bear it. I slaved and tussled to adjust to my new work environment, cleaning up after white people. After six months of anxiety, frustration, and degradation, I quit! This job was not my bag. This is not the American dream I was hoping for. "Now what, Ms. Lee? Let the journey begin."

CHAPTER 1

Uncle Sam Wants You

My mother, bless her heart, always wanted the best for me. Despite being poverty-stricken, this woman, surviving on welfare, by the grace of God found a way to get a loan so I could attend a college twelve miles from my home. She managed to pay back that loan by washing and ironing clothes and cleaning white folk's homes.

I was one proud, happy black camper because no one in my family had gone to College, and I would be back on track in hopes of recapturing my dreams. Initially, I majored in biology and later switched to the teachers' curriculum. For two years, I studied hard, made good grades, and was doing just fine. Something was missing. Did I really want to teach school for the rest of my life? Shucks, no! At age twenty-one, I was missing something more adventurous and challenging. The nagging within was persistent: "What do you want out of life, Lenora? Sit back, think, and figure out just what it is you really want to be in this Promised Land when you grow up."

I began the New Year of 1961 trying to determine what to do with my young life. I dearly appreciated my mother's sacrifices in sending me to college for two years, but I was bored and felt stuck in a depressing small country town that did not look like a Promised Land. One day while strolling the streets of my small town, I curiously entered the army recruiting office where a big poster of a man pointed directly at me saying: UNCLE SAM WANTS YOU. The recruiting sergeant immediately sat me down and began his sales pitch.

"*Lenora, this is your answer for adventure, challenges, education, and travel. You only have to sign up for three years; and since you have two years of college, you can start out as a PFC instead of a private.*"

"*What do I have to do, Sarge, and where will you send me?*" I asked naively.

"*Well, first you'll have to take some written tests and a physical. If you pass, I'll have you sign all the necessary papers. You'll go to Fort McClellan, Alabama, at the Women's Army Corps (WAC) Center for eight weeks of basic training. After you successfully complete this course, you will go to Fort Sam Houston, Texas, for your medical corpsman training. Simple as that,"* Sergeant First Class Burkhardt emphasized.

Exciting thoughts rushed through my youthful mind. I had only been to the states of Maryland, Ohio, West Virginia, and Virginia, so going to Alabama and Texas would indeed become a new experience—much newer than I could ever imagine. Wow, I could travel and see the world, learn a skill, and who knows what else. I didn't even think about discussing this matter with my mother, and before I knew it, I heard my voice speak with enthusiasm, "Okay, Sarge. Tell me what I have to do first."

After completing some paperwork, the sergeant said that he would notify me when I needed to take my test and have a physical examination. I headed for home with my head in the clouds, anxious to tell my mother the good news.

"Mom, I've got to do this. This is my chance to travel and see the world. If I'm accepted into the army, I will do whatever it takes to endure the psychological and physical challenges that I will face during basic training. I will learn in order to grow."

"Do what you need to do. My prayers will be with you," Mom said lovingly.

I passed my written test and physical examination, and within a month, I found myself proudly donning an army uniform, heading for a foreign state, anxiously ready to *be all I can be* in the WAC. I arrived at Anniston, Alabama, in January 1961, during the time of the Selma riots when racial disturbance existed all over the South. I was so naive about racial injustices because I was a protected country kid who grew up in a place where discrimination was not so prevalent. I did not realize I was a woman of color until I set foot on this southern soil and observed racism firsthand. I was traveling from the *ordinary* world to the *extraordinary* world, not knowing what to expect.

As a new recruit in basic, I would be confined to the military post; therefore, I was sheltered from the racism that existed outside the military gate. The Women's Army Corps was an entity in itself that trained its women in a much protected environment separated from the male soldiers. WACs could only receive training in traditional female-type roles (clerical, medical, and supply). The corps was a cohesive, professional female unit that laid the necessary foundation for a young female soldier to excel.

I lived with thirty other females in an open-bay environment with no privacy. We were hustled out of our beds in the early morning hours to begin rigorous physical training, ate three meals a day, attended classes, and cleaned our barracks until lights-out at 10 PM. I associated with females from different states with diverse backgrounds and enhanced my socialization skills. I was older than most of the trainees in my class, who were directly out of high school, so I did not have difficulty taking orders; and discipline became a way of life for me. I was there to learn and be obedient. I took pride in wearing my uniform, readily learned

how to march and drill others, read a compass, survived field training, and enjoyed physical fitness training. I made friends easily and encouraged other trainees who had problems dealing with the emotional and physical stress of basic training. Since I was more mature, disciplined, and adaptive, my drill sergeants consistently chose me for leadership positions.

On my first pass off post, I was startled as I observed the Ku Klux Klan marching unopposed down the main streets of Anniston, a hop, skip, and jump from the army post. I was mystified to discover that blacks could not frequent restaurants or hotels, and that the water fountains and bathrooms were marked Colored and White. I could not identify with the trials and tribulations of the southern black people—I was in a foreign place. This can't be the Promised Land that will permit me to *be all I can be*. The only way I could deal with this unfamiliar discrimination was to be calm and cool and use humor because being hostile and rebellious would only get me into deep trouble.

One evening several of my friends and I decided to go to the drive-in movies. We really didn't think about the consequences and drove off post: three white girls and Ms. Black Lee. When we arrived at the gate, we were refused entrance because I was in the car.

My heart cracked as I heard the attendant say, *"Sorry, ladies. Colored people are not allowed in this drive-in."*

My friends were also shocked, but the driver politely backed out of the entrance and departed. My friends kept apologizing for the embarrassment.

"Gee, Lee, we didn't know. How can they do this to you? We are so sorry about this."

I bit my lips as I responded, *"It's okay. No problem."*

As we headed back to the barracks, I suddenly got this bright idea. *"Hey, let's have some fun with this. I will hide on the floor of the car's back part while you drive back to the drive-in."*

My friends started chuckling and got excited saying, *"That sounds wild. Lee, are you sure you want to do this? This could be dangerous."*

"Heck, yeah! We can't let these prejudiced people get the best of us. Come on. Let's do it?"

The driver turned the car around and headed back to the drive-in as I laid my brown body on the floor. The attendant took a quick glance at the occupants in the car and readily permitted us entrance into the drive-in. We laughed and chuckled over our cockiness in fooling the attendant and had a good time watching the movie. I made sure that nobody could see me from the other cars and was glad that I had a strong bladder.

When we returned to the barracks, my friends kept laughing and talking about the events of the evening and shared the story with others. We had beaten the enemy and infiltrated his space. While lying in my bed that night, I thought about the evening and was very hurt from the bigoted treatment I had suffered in front of my friends. I had used humor to deal with this bias event, but the inhumane treatment tore at my soul deeply. I would never forget that humiliating event in my young life. I was determined that this type of inequity would not affect me as an individual. Despite the color of my skin, I knew that I am just as good as the next person.

H. Lenora Byrd

At the end of basic training, my positive attitude, attributes, and performance paid off. My leaders and peers selected me as the *outstanding trainee* of the cycle. Maybe my dreams of *being all I can be* would not be stifled after all. This was an important turning point in my young life because it showed me that I had unlimited potential. The only direction to go now was *forward and up*. My mother and my recruiting sergeant were very proud of me, and a very nice article about my accomplishments appeared in my small hometown newspaper.

Lesson learned: *Always have a* can do *attitude.* The journey continues as I travel to my next phase of training at Fort Sam Houston, Texas. *What lies ahead of me now?*

CHAPTER 2

Be All You Can Be!

It was time to venture on to my next military challenge for Advanced Individual Training (AIT) as a medical corpsman. I was now on a roll, with visions of an actual Promised Land reeling in my head. I really was not that interested in the medical field; but as a WAC, I did not have too many occupations available to pursue. I shared a room with another enlisted woman, had more privacy than during basic; and there wasn't a platoon sergeant constantly barking at me—I was a human being once again.

I enjoyed my classes and had no problems with the training. I loved to drill and count cadence; therefore, my leaders often selected me to march my classmates to and from classes. My platoon sergeant constantly gave me leadership assignments, which helped me to learn and grow. After I successfully completed my eight weeks of medical training, my first sergeant called me into her office.

"Private First Class Byrd, you've done well in your course, and you've shown me that you are a born leader. I have an offer for you that I know you can't resist."

"And what would that be, First Sergeant?" I asked suspiciously.

"Since you are not too keen on the medical field, how about a job as a platoon sergeant in the detachment? I need someone to keep the Advanced Individual Trainees (AIT) in check, and you know how to handle and drill troops. Plus, I've recommended to the commander that you be given corporal stripes instead of specialist four stripes when you're promoted next week. How about it?"

I was speechless. A platoon sergeant in the '60s was like being a drill sergeant in the '70s. This was a dream of a lifetime. My voice stammered in awe as I spoke. *"Sure, First Sergeant. I'd like that a lot. This is too good to be true."*

I received my corporal stripes and became a platoon sergeant, reveling in pride each time I marched my troops across the post. Moreover, I was now permanent party and had more freedom to come and go as I wished. I began displaying my softball skills when I joined the post slow-pitch softball team and managed to outshine all the players. Slow-pitch was too boring, so I joined a fast-pitch team off post that played semipro softball all around Texas. Pepsi-Cola sponsored the team, and the players were awesome athletes—I received the honor of playing shortstop. Our team even played in a tournament in Mexico City during the 1968 Olympics. Now, this is my bag! I was now a girl athlete, gallivanting throughout the state of Texas on weekends, playing the sport I loved so much.

However, racism was still openly rampant in the South. Frustration and anger overcame me when I, the only black female on the team, constantly experienced discrimination in hotels and restaurants during our softball travels. Nevertheless, my emotions were somewhat softened when my coach and teammates tried to protect me from this racism. They always refused to frequent facilities that discriminated against me. Why treat me so differently because of my skin color? I was not accustomed to this injustice one bit.

I also got lucky, found a group to sing and strum by bass with, and started performing at clubs on and off post. I was being all I could be: a platoon sergeant promoted to sergeant within the year, girl athlete and musician, traveling and experiencing life to the fullest. "There just may be a Promised Land after all," I told myself.

The lovebug struck me when I turned twenty-three. All this time, I have not mentioned any boys in my young life because I had other outlets that were more interesting. During my high school days, boys seemed to be afraid of me and often called me Ms. Iron Petticoat. Ha, ha. "What you see, you cannot touch or have" was my motto during my adolescence. I was having too much fun simply living and exploring to be distracted by the boy species.

Now a little voice was whispering to me: *"Lenora, you'll turn twenty-four soon, and that almost makes you an old maid. You better start thinking about a significant other in your life."* Therefore, out I went with my naive self, trying to deal with the opposite sex. I ended up having a horrible fling with some basketball star, whose name or face I can't even remember. This guy only wanted my body, and I lost my virginity in a very painful and disgusting manner. Thank God, I didn't become pregnant. There was no sense in curling up and crawling into a shell because of this bad sexual experience. Within a short time, I met a handsome tall sergeant named Fred, who was married but separated. I dated him for a whole year, patiently waiting for him to get a divorce.

Again, my first sergeant beckoned me into her office. This time the company commander was present, and I was trying to figure out what I had done wrong. The captain spoke first. *"Sergeant Byrd, you have demonstrated outstanding maturity and leadership potential. Since you have two years of college, the first sergeant and I think you should consider going to Officer Candidate School (OCS) for six months and become a commissioned officer. Are you interested?"*

"Be all you can be" vibrated in my mind as I spoke in a cracked tone. *"I never thought about being an officer, ma'am. I've been enjoying my status as a sergeant."*

"Being a commissioned officer will help you to excel in the military, providing you with bigger challenges and more responsibilities. We feel you are a good candidate for OCS and think you should consider it. We'll help you with the paperwork," the first sergeant said in a persuasive tone.

"The OCS school is at Fort McClellan, right?"

My company commander replied, *"Yes, but if you're worrying about leaving Fort Sam, it will be time for you to ship out to another assignment next year anyway. So don't let that hamper your decision."*

"If you think it's for the best, I'll give it a try," I gasped.

"Okay, we'll start the paperwork immediately. We know you can do it," the first sergeant said reassuringly.

Things were happening very fast. I was given a chance to be an officer—I couldn't wait to share the news with Fred. Surprisingly, he was very encouraging and said that he was considering applying for Warrant Officer School. This meant that we both could become officers. ***Take advantage of any situation that permits you to grow.***

I completed my OCS paperwork and passed all my tests. Within two months, I was headed back to Fort McClellan for six months of extensive training in my newest dream toward becoming an officer. Ironically, when I arrived at WAC Center, my OCS

platoon officer was one of my past AIT trainees at Fort Sam. She also entered the army as an enlistee and later received a direct commission because she was a college graduate. Now she would be in charge of me—I'm glad I treated her well and with respect. 1LT Alice Delgado was an inspiring woman and a professional officer, and I couldn't have asked for a better teacher and mentor. OCS was not as difficult as I expected. I breezed through the six months, continuing to learn, mature, and grow as a person. My mother was very proud as she pinned my butter bars on my uniform in June 1964—her daughter was now a second lieutenant!

Once I left home to venture off into the world, I always felt that I had to do right and excel in the eyes of my mother, who sacrificed so much for me during my early years. Based on my leadership and drill team skills, my superiors convinced me to remain at Fort McClellan as a platoon officer. I jumped at the offer and took my place in one of the highest realms of the WAC—training other women to become officers.

I was in seventh heaven as a platoon officer training other women to become commissioned in the Women's Army Corps. I was now a part of an elite team working with outstanding cadre, great commanding officers, Captain Jump and Major Hinton, and one of my favorite mentors, LT Alice Delgado. Wow, did we have fun training other women to *be all they could be.* During this time frame, I was known by my married name, Lindsey, and Alice tagged me with the nickname Tweety Byrd.

One of my first duties as a new platoon officer in July 1964 was to help train one hundred career-minded young women, representing seventy-one universities and colleges and thirty-three states, in receiving a *taste of army life* at WAC Center. During this particular class, arrangements were made to make a video of me marching the cadets while singing "Jody." I loved to drill and count cadence. The cadets enjoyed this phase of their training, and a nice article was written in the *Army News Photo Feature*, August 1964 about this college junior class. I have no idea what I did in the video!

The WAC College Junior program began at WAC school in 1957. The program ended in 1977 when women began graduating from army ROTC. This four-week course was to familiarize college undergraduates with army life and encourage them to apply for direct commissions. For four weeks each summer (later three), approximately sixty college juniors entered the army as corporals in the army reserve. While on active duty, the army paid for their transportation, gave them the pay and allowances due an E-4, and provided them with uniforms, food, and housing. In return, they attended introductory classes on army organization, leadership, training, administration, close-order drill, and physical training.

This summer's program was directed by LTC Sue Lynch, commanding officer of the U.S. WAC Center and commandant of the school. They also went on field trips to other army posts and worked at WAC Center headquarters, at the Basic Training Battalion, or at WAC school. After the orientation course, they returned to college but remained in the army reserve on inactive duty. Upon graduating from college, they were commissioned as second lieutenants in the army reserve, and they reported on active duty to the WAC Officer Basic course the summer after graduation. Those who did not graduate or declined a commission were simply discharged from the enlistment.

The cadets participated in inspections, parades, company duties, and field exercises. The training given the college juniors was not as rigorous as that given regular officer students, but the faculty was instructed to portray life in the WAC realistically and not to impart any false information or impressions about work, training, additional duties, social life, or career opportunities.

While at Fort McClellan, the cadets, as the college juniors were called, observed the full scope of a WAC officer's life. They also took a three-day trip to Fort Benning, Georgia. After the summer program, the WAC school commandant wrote each participant, sent pictures of her graduation and other events, and wished her luck in her senior year. The commandant also wrote the dean of women or dean of students, whichever was appropriate, to describe the program and the student's participation in it and to send photographs. After three years in the army, I found myself marching rapidly up the mountaintop toward my envisioned Promised Land. I was *being all that I could be* when suddenly I created a gigantic valley that drastically changed my journey forever.

CHAPTER 3

Valley Time

After successfully completing OCS, I made a choice that would immensely affect my military career. Fred finally got his divorce; we married in October 1964; however, he was not accepted to Warrant Officer School. During this period, it was taboo for an officer to marry an enlisted person, which the army considered to be fraternization. My superiors quickly called me before the carpet and shared their oppositions with me.

"Lieutenant Lindsey, the army frowns upon fraternization between commissioned and noncommissioned officers," the female colonel barked.

"Ma'am, I was engaged to this soldier before I became an officer."

"Regardless, you've made a big mistake by marrying an enlisted man," she responded in a command voice.

I departed her office as my emotions became enraged. *How could the military dictate who you can or cannot fall in love with and/or marry?*

Rage and confusion continued to burn inside as I tried to think rationally on what to do next. Fred was also livid and kept telling me that the army does not have the right to interfere in our personal lives. The more I pondered on the subject, the angrier I got. I had no problems obeying military rules and regulations that made sense, but this was preposterous. The decision I made resulted in the first steps to claiming my individuality and becoming a nonconformist. I refused to let any system decree what I could or could not do in my personal life—I will preserve my personal identity.

I continued my job as a platoon officer at McClellan, while Fred remained at Fort Sam. Within the year, I received orders for Orleans, France, and to my shock, I was pregnant. Pregnant women could not serve in the military during this time frame. I had thrown my pregnant black body into a big-time valley! There was no way for me to fight and win this battle as I watched the dirt pile quickly over me, lying futilely in my self-made hole.

My superiors, who seemed pleased, informed me that I had to resign my commission by the end of the year. My rose-colored dreams had become a drastic, dark nightmare that completely changed the course of my life's journey. My military career was coming to an abrupt end, and there wasn't a thing I could do about it. I hung my head in humbling defeat as I slowly transformed from a confident, high self-esteemed person to a worried, scared, and confused person. I had made my own bed, and now I had to flounder in it trying to determine what to do next.

In October 1965, I submitted my resignation with stiff dignity and a deflated ego. I swallowed the choking despair in my throat as I ended my time in the army—three months before promotion to first lieutenant. I returned to Texas to be with my husband and attempted to start my life all over again as a civilian. Once my emotions dissipated, I began thinking soberly and refused to give up hope. I was going to have a child in five months, leaving me time to still be active and productive. Sitting at home watching the soaps while Fred worked was not going to do a thing for me. "So, Lee, get a job and keep busy until the baby is due." I contacted my old softball coach, who was also the manager of the Pepsi-Cola plant and told him my situation.

"Hey, Lee. I'll give you a job even though you can't play softball for us. Come by and see me as soon as you can."

I felt a sense of relief as I echoed, *"Thanks, Coach. I really appreciate this."* **When life kicks me in the behind, let it kick me forward!**

A ray of hope began beaming within my soul. I accepted a job as a bottle checker at the plant; and within a short time, I was almost back to my old bubbly self. My daughter kept kicking inside as if she wanted out of my womb ahead of time. By my ninth month, I was getting fat as a rat—sixty pounds had taken over my previous 135-pound shapely thin frame. This was going to be one big baby. My husband, an avid golfer, asked me to accompany him on the course one Saturday, so I agreed. I needed the exercise, so I walked eighteen holes of golf with him on a nice, sunny Texas afternoon and felt exuberant once we returned home.

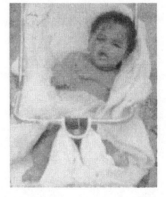

The next day it decided to snow in San Antonio; snow flurries in February is unheard of for this city. Well, guess who decided she wanted to make her exit on this snowy white day? After four excruciating hours in labor and cursing my husband for putting me through all the discomfort, it was finally over. I gave birth to a screaming eight-pound, eight-ounces curly black-haired daughter with sparkling jet-black eyes, and smooth bronze skin. Ms. Chantay was the most beautiful baby I had ever seen. She was indeed very precious, and I soon forgot about all the pain I went through to bring her into this world. Fred was one proud daddy, and Mom was an elated grandmother.

Everything happens for a reason. Each time I held my precious baby, her dark, radiant eyes penetrated my soul. The spirit within kept telling me that my past actions were justified and destined. I was meant to have this child, even at the expense of ending my military career. God is good, and I thanked him for a healthy, bouncing blessed baby. *In every lesson, God sends me a blessing.*

I took my baby girl home, started learning how to care for her; and for the very first time, I actually lived with my husband. Things were going smoothly for about a month, when I noticed that Fred was not the dependable husband and father I expected. He was obsessed with golf, flashy clothes, and his luxury car. Suddenly, there was no food in the house and no money to buy baby items for my newborn. I was married to a sergeant first class with lavish tastes, who didn't have a pot to pee in. Fred was irresponsible and far from being a family man and breadwinner. Grief and despair tore through my heart as I realized that I could not live like this. I saw another ditch creeping my way. "Lord, help me. Please show me the way."

Well, this time I was not going to wait for the ditch to transpose into a valley. I told Mr. Fred I was going to get a job and make my own money to live on. I would ensure that my child was properly cared for and not neglected. I called my mother and asked her if she would take care of the baby, while I went in search of a job. Mom agreed, and she flew to Texas to get Chantay. I hit the San Antonio streets in search of a job, knowing that my mother would take exceptional loving care of my daughter.

I worked as a cartographer for a while, and then a softball friend referred me to the department of recreation. They hired me as a recreational specialist working with poor children in a Mexican-American ghetto area. It did not matter to me what Fred did or did not do. I reclaimed my independence and became self-sufficient once again. He did his thing, and I continued working and playing softball and music. I was marching forward to the sound of a very different drumbeat. *A burden can become a bridge to a new life and a new me.*

Within the next two years, I was preparing my *Dear John* speech for Fred, when he suddenly got orders for Vietnam. I decided not to be cruel, kept the divorce thoughts to myself, and wished him safety in the war zone. He was going to be a military advisor during the initial stages of the war, which kept him out of harm's way. I wasted no time packing up my belongings and headed home to be with my daughter and mother, whom I missed very much. It was so good to see Chantay, who was now a chubby spry fun-loving two-year-old. She was fat! Mom and the neighbors were feeding her turnip and collard greens, rice and gravy, ribs, chicken—the works.

It was time for me to get back into action and make plans for moving ahead while my husband was out of my life. I had GI educational benefits, so I returned to my alma mater to complete my bachelor's degree. What a journey. I was right back where I left off after graduating from high school. During the next year and a half, I was again making progress without any evidence of obstacles. Then Fred notified me that he was returning to the States with an assignment in Washington, DC. I really felt guilty because I had not missed his presence in my life. So Fred appeared on our doorstep and spent his leave time with us. How could I convince this man that our marriage was over?

Fred played the proud daddy and attempted to get back into my good graces as I tried to avoid being tricked and trapped into his personal agenda. Chantay and I were doing just fine; and I had my own plans, which did not include going to Walter Reed where Fred was going to be a golf instructor. What a nice, smooth military life this man had. *God takes care of fools and babies.*

You would think that I had learned a worthwhile lesson about love and marriage. My innate female instincts kept yelling at me, *This marriage ain't gonna work, girl. You're almost finished with college. Don't let this man get you offtrack again.* Nevertheless, what did I do? Overwhelmed with guilt, I gave in, put my plans on hold, and opted to give Fred another shot at our marriage. This time Chantay was going with us, and he was going to take adequate care of the family or else. He humbly agreed, and off we went to DC. Fred found a small apartment that was not to my liking, but I had to give him a chance.

I decided to find a job and went to the DC department of recreation to see if they offered a similar position that I had in San Antonio; DC had playgrounds everywhere. So I put in my application for a recreation specialist; and based on my background, I immediately got a job at a playground located in a ghetto area. I took Chantay to work with me every day and let her play with the other kids, as I supervised all playground activities. Gang members frequented the playground, but they didn't give me too much grief based on my authoritative military demeanor. Some of the older gang members even helped with the kids on the playground.

I had my own life and income, just in case Fred would not hold up his part of the bargain. He was a good guy who meant well, but I had certain expectations. I wanted happiness, security, and needed to raise my child as best I could; but he was into his golf and simply didn't seem to notice we were drifting apart. He continued to be lavish, self-centered, and irresponsible toward family matters. My love life was miserable and intolerable, and it was time for me to make my exit. Marriage was not the life for me.

When I finally told Fred that our marriage was over and that I was leaving him, he became a madman to the point of physical abuse. I'm sorry, but God did not give me this body for a man to use as a punching bag. His abusive action solidified my decision—I'm outta here! This marriage is over. After being with Fred for four years, there was nothing good left to remember about our relationship. I married because I thought it was the right thing to do at the time, but I did not want or need a man in my life. I am glad it did not take me forever to realize such. I made a mistake, and it was time to rectify it. For the next few months, Fred kept trying to convince me to stay in the marriage and continued acting like a madman.

I got a court restraining order to keep him from bothering Chantay and me. After this action, Fred eventually gave up; and we had our day in court. I received a separation, to the point of not requiring him to pay child support. If he didn't support Chantay while we were married, why would he do it if we were separated? Fred finally disappeared from my life, and I was freed from misery and obstacles that the marriage brought. Enough is enough.

Years later, I discovered that Fred got out of the army and returned to his home state. I kept my married name, Lindsey, for my daughter's sake and changed back to my maiden name, Byrd, in 1988 before I retired from the army. I ensured that Chantay had access to all of his pictures, his forwarding address and phone number, if she ever wanted to contact her father. I was free from the shackles that bound me, and it was time for me to begin my new life. A unique journey awaits me as I proceed on this new path. *Where would it lead me?*

CHAPTER 4

Entertaining and in the Life

The societal myth that says "A woman needs a man in her life" became a blatant, downright-rotten lie for me. Not only did I pull the plug on Fred, but on society as well. I neither wanted nor needed a man in my life to feel *complete*. Conforming to societal mores and rules was not the right formula for me. My new transformation was blasting forth like a lightning rod—straight life was over for me. Was I born gay, or was I the victim of my upbringing, of my family composition, of my worldly experiences, or of my propensity to be independent and self-reliant? Did I suffer some awful illness, or did I just discover the *real me?* My latent gay tendencies finally kicked in at age twenty-eight, and I increasingly started noticing women.

Lesbians seemed to be everywhere in DC: my immediate boss, my beautician, softball players, and musicians. My first relationship was with Joan, my recreation center boss and the person who stood by me when my husband became abusive. I took Chantay back to her grandmother's in Pennsylvania and moved in with Joan. I continued playing softball, working, and made extra cash playing music. After six months or so, my various activities and my role on the home front eventually seemed to concern my new lover. She was from the *old gay* school where lesbians played roles. Joan wanted to be the *butch* and felt that I was supposed to play the *femme* role.

"You've got to be kidding, Joan. What's with this role-playing?" I blurted out.

"I'm used to having a femme lover who cooks, cleans, and takes good care of me. You're always out in the streets playing softball or music. I want a femme!"

I almost chuckled to myself. Joan was petite, who had delusions of being a big bad lesbian butch. I guess my towering tall body intimidated her, and my independent nature was not to her liking. I was very naive about gay life, which in the '60s and '70s seemed to revolve around lesbians being either *butch* or *femme*. Refusing to conform to any role-playing, my response to Joan was *"Well, honey pie, I just got rid of a man. I did not become your lover in search of a woman trying to be a man. You'll have to accept me the way I am because I'm not changing, dear. You better go find yourself a so-called femme because I'm out of here!"*

I cried over this breakup for at least one day and rapidly moved on to greener pastures containing more interesting challenges and attractive women. I remained in the DC/Maryland area and accidentally found myself involved in a potential music career. I quit my recreation job because I didn't think it was wise to be around Joan. I moved to my own apartment, used my GI bill again, and enrolled in law enforcement courses at the University of Maryland in College Park.

I also worked part-time as a campus police officer, and my boss decided to give me an assignment guarding some woman named Janis Joplin, who was scheduled to perform at the college. He selected me because I was the only female on the force. I never heard of this woman, who I later discovered was a well-known white blues singer. I assumed my duties as this singer's personal bodyguard, followed her around the dressing room, and watched over her as she performed. I was not impressed with this white woman, who was vulgar, arrogant, and drank too much Southern Comfort. I was sorely displeased when I heard her sing: only black folks knew how to sing the blues. Despite her stardom, it was obvious this was a very sad and unhappy woman. She was out of it during her concert performance, either from alcohol or drugs. Within a few months, this woman was found dead in some dreary room from a drug overdose. A very sad ending, indeed.

After hearing Joplin's performance, I thought to myself, *Hey, I can do that as well as play the bass guitar. What's this woman got that I don't have?* When the concert was over, I spoke to one of the entertainer promoters—a tall, copper-skinned man with a smooth bald head. I told him about my musical background, and he said he would arrange for me to audition with a group in Baltimore. Sure enough, he followed through, and I enthusiastically drove to Baltimore for an audition. The group already had a bass player, but I was picked up as a singer. Our ten-piece band, the Renaud Junction, comprised of five musicians and five singers, and our distinctive sound was awesome

as the music and the five voices blended so harmoniously. Our performance was an act to behold as we dressed up in lively, colorful, flashy costumes and worked out our own choreography. We became very popular and began performing in a Baltimore nightclub six days a week. I quit my college job so that I could do the thing I loved the most-entertain full-time. Our band members moved into a communal

setting where we ate, slept, rehearsed, made candles, and lived our lives for more than a year. I found my true calling—music and entertaining. I also came out of my closet with a bang and was now *in the life.* As an entertainer, women seemed to flock to my feet. Gay folks were everywhere!

I did not have time for a serious relationship because I was sowing my oats and singing my lungs and heart out in the name of pleasure and enjoyment. These gay experiences aided me in learning more about my own body—my erogenous zones, what I liked and didn't like in intimacy. Being intimate with a woman brought more warmth, tenderness, compassion, and a lack of inhibition. I never experienced these elements with a man; I acknowledged and accepted my chosen lifestyle and sexual orientation.

I met so many different people and had a variety of growing experiences during my entertaining days and adaptation to being *in the life.* It was the era of marijuana, but I did not need a drug to make me high because I had my own innate, natural high, especially when I played music. Two of the male band members were gay, and we bonded well together. Our band was so good that our manager booked us for a summer job at Ocean City, Maryland, where we met and performed with Diana Ross and the Jackson 5. Our performances resulted in our manager obtaining a contract to record an album with the Motown label to include performing as the opening act for the Jackson 5.

Michael Jackson was a very shy thirteen-year-old, who was closely protected by his parents and agents. I never had a one-on-one with this youngster, who became the top performing pop star of our time. Our band went on a three-month entertaining tour with the renowned group, traveling through the South and Midwest states. We were well received as the opening act, and we knew our album would be a winner once it hit the market. Stardom for our band was on the horizon when an unanticipated devil reared its ugly head.

After the tour, our manager went to Motown to finalize our album contract. Lo and behold, he never returned to Baltimore. We sat for weeks waiting for his return, only to discover that he made a deal for himself rather than for the group. He left us hanging with no contract, no album, and no stardom. It never crossed our minds that our manager would be disloyal to us. Our musical hopes and dreams came to a devastating climax, leaving us baffled and frustrated. Our motivation and incentive for entertaining quickly dissipated; we dissolved our group and tearfully went our separate ways. We gave up. So much talent wasted because of someone else's personal greed. What would have happened if our group had a loyal and honest manager?

I licked my salty wounds and accepted the fact that at age thirty I was not going to be a well-known musician and entertainer. Once again, my visions drifted faintly into the clouds with another drastic turning point in my life. Another valley fell into my path, restricting a successful journey in my perceived Promise Land. I lost count as to how many strikes I had accumulated in my ball game of misfortune. There was no other choice but to pack up and head home to decide my next step. A flash of dark grief rippled within as I surrendered to defeat and reflected on my past journey. My upward-bound military career came to a hasty, devastating end because of my decision to get married. Marriage presented me with an unpleasant dilemma; I had to fight my way out of it and begin my new lifestyle. Then my true love—dreams of a music career—came to an unexpected, heartfelt crash. *What if* I had taken other courses of action?

It was apparent that growing meant taking risks, enduring the strife, but never giving up hope. Despite the setbacks and the *what ifs*, I had to humbly learn each lesson, regroup, and attempt to move forward. My mysterious journey had to continue with hope and faith replacing any despair.

One who risks nothing does nothing, has nothing, and is nothing.

CHAPTER 5

Unfinished Business

Whatever events occurred during my military journey is in direct correlation to what I needed to learn in life. It was now time to heal, meditate, contemplate, regroup, and decide upon a plan. I returned home and was glad to be back with my family. Mom had taken such good care of lively chubby Chantay while I was off trying to find my place in the music world. I was so blessed to have such a wonderful, caring mother who not only supported me but also understood me.

It was time to determine my next step. I had not completed my degree because of my decision to remain with my husband; so once again, I enrolled in college. I continued my major in social work and did my practicum at the local child welfare agency located in Uniontown. I also took a gigantic step by joining the army reserves. In July 1973, I enlisted with the 430th Replacement Detachment located in Hiller, with the rank of specialist 5; and a woman had never been assigned to this reserve unit. The military was still in my blood; and despite the rank, I enjoyed my monthly weekend drill. I had another vision and a plan; I was going to get a direct commission as a first lieutenant in the U.S. Army Reserve once I attained my bachelor's degree.

After a year and a half, I received my BS degree in social work; it had taken me twelve years to get a degree, but I finally did it. I was hired as a full-time caseworker with child welfare services and ventured on a new mission to find foster and adoption homes for young black children in my community.

I applied for a direct commission as a first lieutenant in the army reserves and got it. I was sworn in by 1LT Malcolm Campbell, commanding officer of the detachment, and received congratulations from First Sergeant William Gordon. I accomplished my set goals; and after seven years being out of the army, I attained the rank I would have received if I had not been required to resign in 1965. *Life cannot get better until you get better!*

I was an officer once again and began having thoughts of my positive experiences during my past time in the army. I contacted Sherian Cadoria, a dear friend and mentor who became WAC's first black female one-star general. It had been years since I talked to her and she was now a major. During our conversation, she gave me information on the recent changes in the army as it applied to women with children.

"Lee, the laws on women with children in the military changed in 1972. You can return to active duty as a first lieutenant, if you are willing to have your mother assume custody of your daughter."

PROMOTED TO FIRST LT. — H. Lenora Lindsey is shown being sworn in as a first lieutenant by First Lt. Malcolm Campbell, commanding officer of the 430th Replacement Detachment, U.S. Army Reserve, Hiller, while First Sergeant William Gordon of the company looks on. Lt. Lindsey will serve for two years as a company commander in one of the units at the WAC Training Center at Ft. McClellan, Ala. The lieutenant enlisted with the 430th Replacement Detachment on July 3, 1973, and was given the rank of Specialist 5. She previously served for four and one-half years in the Army as a lieutenant before being discharged from the service. Following her enlistment in the Reserve she re-applied for her commission and received it. She originally enlisted in the WAC through the U.S. Army Recruiting Station in Unlelaw. The daughter of Eunice Byrd, LaBelle, Lt. Lindsey is the mother of an eight-year-old daughter, Chantay.

"That sounds tempting, but I would have to start all over from scratch. All of my OCS classmates are now captains and majors."

"So what if you're behind the power curve? You can do it, Lee. You are a born leader, and I think the military is your calling. If you decide to pursue this, I'll help you get back on active duty."

I responded humbly, *"Okay. Let me discuss this with my mother. I'll call you back. Thanks for the input, my dearest friend."*

"You're more than welcome. Come back in; I miss having you around. We need more black female officers in this army. Take care and I'll talk to you later."

I discussed the situation with my mother, who agreed to support me in whatever I decided to do. The more I pondered, the more vivid the answer: This was about *unfinished business* in my life—a career and a mysterious journey that I started twelve years ago that needed to be completed. Now was not the time to give up. I had to accept returning to the army as a challenge and pursue a new goal. My military quest began at the young age of twenty-one, was cut short at age twenty-five; and now at age thirty-three, I made my decision. I contacted Major Cadoria, told her that I was ready to return on active duty; and she said that she would assist me with the necessary paperwork.

In April 1974, I headed back to Fort McClellan with a duty assignment as commander of Company C, Third WAC Basic Training Battalion. Upon my arrival, I was presented with Charlie, the black goat mascot of the company. Charging Charlie was quite possibly the only male who was a bona fide member of the Women's Army Corps during this time. He was discovered by some trainees when his mother disowned him; he was the black goat on the farm. The trainees then took him to their graduation party, where he was admired by all; and ever since, he became *the* Charlie of Charlie company. SGT Nancy Hill and 2LT Georgia Stahle became keepers of the goat and took very good care of him. Charlie's pen was officially dedicated May 2, 1974, when LTC Nelda Cade cut the ribbon to his new home. The Fort McClellan newspaper took a picture of me feeding Charlie grass with a nice article about him. Such great memories; I wonder what happened to Charging Charlie.

The WAC was still serving as a separate unit but was scheduled for disbandment in the next four years (1978). The time for integration into the all-man army was in the making. During my previous days at McClellan, I never bothered to query if anyone was gay or not. Now it was hitting me smack in the face. Women were living together prudently and performing their duties honorably. Military police investigators were conducting gay *witch hunts*, but people were not telling. The "don't ask, don't tell" policy was not in effect during this time frame, but somehow gays managed to discreetly maintain their gender orientation.

I will not pursue this subject in depth in this book because I do not want to expose or offend any of my past lovers, military friends, and acquaintances. The bottom line is that *homosexuality* was and is prevalent in the armed forces. They have and are dying for their country just as their straight military counterparts. One's sexual orientation will not dissipate into the sunset; so face it—it's here to stay.

I was back in the army doing what I do best—training others to become the *best they can be*. Because of my seven-year break in service, I was much older than my peers; and I was usually the same age as many of my superiors. I was behind the power curve in rank, but there wasn't a thing I could do about it. I just may have bit off more than I could chew, and this was going to be a hard mountain to climb.

My battalion commander, a tall Texan woman who spoke with a slow but decisive drawl, was a very good boss who assisted me in adapting rapidly. I had conscientious, work-driven drill sergeants and cadre, who professionally trained and took good care of the basic recruits. They loved competing with the other three companies and the two other WAC battalions. Unfortunately, our battalion was scheduled for deactivation within ten months, and I would be assigned as a company commander in a different battalion. My battalion commander, LTC Ruth Cade, gave me two outstanding officer evaluation reports (OER), which is the military tool used to rate soldiers on their performance and potential for advancement. As I read my OERs, I realized that I had not lost my touch as a person and a leader.

"Lieutenant Lindsey, a returnee to the army after a seven-year service break, acted with a maturity uncommon to others of her grade and with a fresh approach and innovative spirit . . . She has an outgoing personality, which allowed her to establish immediate rapport and to communicate effectively with those at all levels of command . . . Despite her heavy workload, she contributes to the recreational and social activities of the post. She is an outstanding individual and should be considered for early promotion to the next higher grade."

My departing OER was also outstanding: *"Lieutenant Lindsey is one of the most effective unit commanders I have worked with. Her innovations work because she is constantly involved in planning and directing the activities of her unit. She is also perceptive and understanding of human nature. Due to deactivation of the battalion, she will be reassigned to continue her able performance as a company commander. To maximize her potential to the army, early attendance at the military police (MP) advanced course is recommended. She is an outstanding individual and should be considered for early promotion to the next higher grade."*

I was very pleased with my evaluations, but there was no time to pat myself on the back. I was heading to a new battalion with new game rules from a new boss: a woman with cold eyes, a husky voice, and a mouth, tight and grim, absent of any smiles. I felt a storm brewing and heading my way, waiting to blow my brown body into a ditch. This lieutenant colonel was the complete opposite of my previous commander, and my female intuition told me that she and I were not going to hit it off. I will refrain from using her real name.

During the past ten months, I became very well-known and liked on post. My leadership attributes and my talents as a musician and a softball player spoke for themselves. I formed an all-female band with musicians from the WAC band, coached and played softball for the post team, and received recognition accordingly. These extracurricular activities and my popularity did not seem to fare well with my new boss, Lieutenant Colonel Brown.

I had just successfully traveled out of a path of radiant light right into a dark, dreary dungeon. I had to start all over again as a commander for a woman who made it very obvious that she disliked me. However, I was not going to be shoved into a hole by some woman who had personal hang-ups. I would simply do my job and not let her get the better of me. During my second month in command, I seriously injured my knee playing tag football and had an operation to remove a torn cartilage. I hobbled around my company and training sites on crutches for several months. Despite the injury, I still did my job and tried to ignore the unfair treatment from my boss. I was older than her three other company commanders and quickly established rapport with my cadre. My company excelled in all competitions and displaced the high ratings once held by another company that captured Lieutenant Colonel Brown's partiality.

For the next seven months, I could do no right in the eyes of Lieutenant Colonel Brown. When it was time for my annual OER, this woman tried to stab me in the back with her black military pen. The OER of the 1970s was based on a numerical rating, and the rater and endorser had narrative blocks for commenting on a soldier's performance of duty. The rater and endorser could award a total of one hundred points each for a sum total of two hundred. My last two OERs were 196 and 197 consecutively. Lieutenant Colonel Brown's total on my OER was ninety out of one hundred allotted. My past commander's totals were ninety-eight and ninety-nine. How could I drop so low at performance and potential ratings within seven months? I was flabbergasted as I read the low evaluation. I maxed out on all my professional attributes—moral and character strength, technical competence, judgment, communication, personal conduct, innovativeness, responsibility, and physical fitness.

However, on demonstrated performance of duty, she gave me sixty-six out of seventy; and on potential for advancement, she gave me twenty-four out of thirty. In the mandatory narrative block, she wrote three low-keyed sentences about my performance that covered half of the block. It wasn't what she said that mattered, but rather what she didn't say. Her failure to provide a complete narrative in the block stood out like a sore thumb. It was time for my first military battle, so I donned my armor, put on my fighting gloves, determined not to take this injustice lying down.

I confronted Lieutenant Colonel Brown, one-on-one, saying, *"Colonel, I refuse to sign this OER. I don't understand how I can go from two outstanding ratings of ninety-eight and ninety-nine from my past commander, and you only gave me a ninety. This is not right."*

She coldly remarked, *"Well, I'm different than your past commander; therefore, I rate differently."*

"Colonel, you didn't even bother to complete the narrative block. It's obvious that you have something against me, so I am submitting an appeal to higher authorities. I will not accept or sign this OER as is," I said in an authoritative voice.

"Do as you please, but I will not change my rating," she blurted out.

This woman was callous, coldhearted, and striving to defeat me. I furiously departed her office and headed straight to the WAC commandant's office. Colonel Heinz was a very pleasant, well-respected, compassionate officer. I showed her my OER and explained my rationale for appealing.

"I think I know what the problem is here. I'll take care of this. You just continue doing your work, and I'll get back to you," she said with a reassuring tone.

"Ma'am, whatever you say. However, after this is resolved, I think it's time for me to move on. I will never be able to work for Lieutenant Colonel Brown again."

"I understand how you feel. Let me see if we can get you assigned to the Military Police (MP) School. The brigade commander knows you well, so I'm sure he can assist us."

"That will be great. Thank you, ma'am."

I departed her office feeling a little better and did as she suggested. Within the week, I was beckoned to the commandant's office.

"Lieutenant Lindsey, I have the final copy of your OER. Lieutenant Colonel Brown refused to change her rating, so I endorsed your OER; and the general added his comments. Here is your copy to read."

A pit formed in my abdomen as I took the OER and read the commandant's rating: *"My perception and personal observation of Lieutenant Lindsey's performance is that she had confidence in her trainers and gave them room to function outstandingly. Her own optimism and enthusiasm reflected in her troops who were always of high morale and esprit, yet well disciplined. Without exception, her company excelled in all areas of its training mission. I attribute this to her fine leadership and administrative skill. My ranking of Lieutenant Lindsey in a higher category than the rater is based on my knowledge of the differing* modus operandi *of the rater and rated officer. Lieutenant Lindsey was transferred from a deactivated battalion whose outstanding commander operated in a totally different manner from the rater. Lieutenant Lindsey reflects the former commander's methods. Although not fully accommodating to the new commander's ways, she has continued to exhibit great talent—musically, professionally, and in human relations. She shares these talents and has enriched the entire community. She has great potential for the army and should be developed accordingly."*

I turned the page and read the general's (male post commander) remarks: *"I agree with the comments of the endorsing officer. Lieutenant Lindsey has performed her duties in an outstanding manner and has the potential to be an outstanding commander or staff officer in the army. I strongly recommend her promotion ahead of her contemporaries."*

A sign of relief came after reading the OER. Colonel Heinz gave me 97 points and my total was 187 out of 200—ten points less than my last OER.

The colonel responded meekly. *"This is the best we can do. The general and I think that our comments will buffer the rater's remarks."*

"It was all about my not being a yes *person and my popularity on post, wasn't it?"*

"Well, it definitely seems that Lieutenant Colonel Brown was not used to a more mature and actively involved officer as you. She is used to mentoring others, and you were beyond that. But don't worry about it. You will be okay. I've made arrangements for you to meet with the MP brigade commander who is very interested in having you on his side of the post."

"Thank you for your assistance, Colonel."

"You're welcome. You should be contacted by the MP school soon."

I slowly made my departure, still feeling uneasy about the overall rating. Lieutenant Colonel Brown's remarks and low rating would still be in my personnel file. Lieutenant Colonel Brown became livid when she had to sign my final OER and resented not being supported by the colonel and the general. I was indeed nothing like her other younger commanders, and she failed to respect me as a person of maturity and wisdom. It's a shame that a superior in the military has the ability to ruin a professional subordinate soldier with the stroke of a pen. ***Stand my ground and fight all injustices that plague me!***

I barely managed to survive sixteen months at WAC Center, but this would be my final assignment as a member of the Women's Army Corps. I quickly arranged for a transfer to the military police side of the installation. The corps would disband soon, and female officers were told to start deciding what occupation they wanted to pursue. A majority of the WACs had already opted to retire, join the reserves, and refused to accept the integration of women into the all-man army. We could choose any branch except combat arms (infantry, armor, artillery, etc.). Since my military life was already a struggling battle, the last thing on my mind was becoming a combat soldier. I decided that being a military police combat support officer was good enough for me. It was time to move on and integrate with the male soldiers and try to play catch-up in my new branch as best I could. Now the real fun is about to begin! *Oh, Lord, please be with me!*

CHAPTER 6

The All-Man Army

The WAC Center would no longer be in existence in the next two years, and women were now getting the opportunity to be a *first guinea pig* in the new male-oriented army. Various occupations were opening up for women: commanders of male units, firing weapons, field training with men, airborne training, and various duties that only men were permitted to perform. My assignment to the MP school would be a different challenge: integration into an unknown private male military Promised Land. **When one door closes, a new one opens!** As chief of the Firearms Training Committee, I was

responsible for supervising fourteen NCOs (noncommissioned officers) and operating two small arms (.45-caliber pistols) and a shotgun range for MPs attending the eight-week AIT program. I jumped headfirst into this new and exciting job and developed doctrine and implemented new training procedures. For four months, I did an outstanding job and was well liked by the MP brigade commander, who offered me an upward mobility position

as an instructor at the MP school. I received an outstanding OER and was back on track after my battle with Lieutenant Colonel Brown. *"Lieutenant Lindsey, a mature, professional soldier, willingly sought additional responsibilities and consistently accomplished her assigned duties efficiently with minimum supervision . . . She has outstanding potential for advancement within the military."*

My next job as an instructor presented me with a definite challenge in the workplace as well as personally. My immediate supervisor was a black male officer, and he and I were close in age. I will refrain from using his real name. Major

Smith initially assisted me in getting settled into my duties as a civil disturbance instructor to senior civilian law enforcement officers and high-ranking military personnel. The popular four-week course was offered during an era when civil disturbance was occurring throughout the States and on military posts. The course was completely foreign to me, and I had to get my act together quickly because I instructed civilian police chiefs and military personnel who outranked me. These men would try to intimidate me based on my sex and rank. I spent numerous off duty hours researching my subject, reviewing old lesson plans, and eventually felt confident and knowledgeable of my subject. These grumpy old know-it-all men tried to eat me alive in the classroom, but I stood my ground and beat them at their game. I maintained a "can do" attitude and refused to accept less than outstanding performance for myself. I quickly developed a high level of expertise in the civil disturbance field, presented it in a competent manner, and received respect and admiration from my classes.

However, I was confronted with a little trench placed in my path by Major Smith when he tried to use his rank and position as a means of seduction. Not everyone on post knew about my sexual orientation, and I always conducted myself in a discreet professional feminine manner. Major Smith, who was not the most handsome man in the world, insisted upon trying me with his seductive power play. I finally got fed up with his pursuits and pulled him aside in the office for a one-on-one thrashing. I learned from experience that it was wiser to confront a superior without any witnesses.

"Come on. Can't you see that I'm interested in you? I can help your career a lot if you cooperate," he said with a quirky smile on his face.

"Look, man. What makes you think I find you attractive? You're married, and I'll mess you up if you don't back off," I warned in a serious tone.

The more I protested, the more he seemed to get turned on. This ugly, disgusting man was pushing me up against a wall, and I had no time to put up with his advances. I was trying to do my job.

"My wife doesn't have to know anything about this. You never know; you just may enjoy it," he responded with a lustful grin.

I finally lashed out in a forceful voice, *"Major, you can't go around treating black sisters like we are a piece of meat. I'll be damned if I'm going to let you disrespect me. You better leave me alone and seriously think about your wife and kids. Otherwise, I'll put a hurt on you that you'll never forget. So back off, now!"*

And that he did, because no doubt he could see in my eyes and hear it in my voice that I was not playing his game. From that day on, I never had any more problems with Major Smith. I demanded his respect and I got it.

For five months, I truly enjoyed my job as an instructor, and my self-esteem and confidence level were greatly enhanced with this experience. After promotion to captain, it was time to move on to another job with more responsibilities. It reminded me of my past days of progress as an enlisted woman, who quickly became an officer. If only I wasn't behind the rank curve, things would have been more satisfying.

A sense of accomplishment engulfed me as I read my departing OER, the majority of which was written by my shunned pal, Major Smith: *"Captain Lindsey would be an asset to any organization and could be counted on to give 100 percent. This attribute is substantiated by the fact that 80 percent of her instruction was presented to law enforcement officials with an average of twenty years experience, and her creditability was never challenged. She gained an unusually high degree of respect from senior law enforcement students and has demonstrated high potential for service in higher grades."*

The MP brigade commander called me to his office with an offer I couldn't resist. *"Captain Lindsey, your performance and leadership skills this past year has been outstanding. How would you like to be a first? I think you would make a fantastic company commander, so I want you to be one of the first women to take on this challenge. How about it?"*

"You want me to command an MP company, sir?" I asked in awe.

"Yes, an AIT unit. After successfully standing up against the older law enforcement officers, handling an enlisted male staff should be a piece of cake for you. Plus I'm going to assign you to one of my best battalion commanders, Lieutenant Colonel Adams, who will ensure you get a fair shake," he responded with reassurance.

"I truly respect Lieutenant Colonel Adams, and it would be a privilege to work for him. When do I start, Colonel?"

"You will have to wait until the present commander ends his tour in six months. That seems like a long time, but I want you to be patient until he departs. Until then, I have a project officer job that will keep you busy."

"Okay, sir. I'll be patient and thank you for considering me for this challenge."

My short-term job turned out to be very boring since it was a research project—a desk job. I missed interacting with people and troops, but I hung in there as I awaited command. My bosses were all white male majors and lieutenant colonels, who appeared to resent yet tolerate me, knowing that I had backing from the MP brigade commander. I avoided any clashes with them, did my job as best I could, and gladly departed this job with a good OER: *"Captain Lindsey is a diligent, industrious officer with a pleasing personality that enabled her to work well with others. She is physically fit and mentally able to meet demanding jobs in a stressful environment. Because of these capabilities, she is being assigned as a company commander within the MP brigade, a most competitive professional environment. Recommend immediate MP Officer Advanced (MPOA) course attendance."*

I performed military police duties for the past year without having any experience or the basic foundations. As an MP 2LT, an officer is supposed to complete the MP Basic course before performing any type of MP duties, but I had too much rank to go through this course and was eligible for the MPOA devised for 1LTs and captains. This course was supposed to teach me how to perform higher levels of duties as an MP officer, even though I had surpassed that level of responsibility. I would have to wait to attend the advance course after I completed my command—*the cart came before the horse.*

Based on my leadership abilities and mature attitude demonstrated at WAC Center and the MP brigade, I became a *first* in doing things out of sync. Being a black female officer was beginning to have its rewards. In essence, I became a *token* for the all-man MP army that was willing to let me be a first so I could put a feather on their caps. This was all right for me because I was willing to serve this role as long as I was treated fairly. *Take advantage of any situation that gives me the opportunity to learn and grow.*

And that I did during the next year of my command. I enjoyed this job and became a part of implementing the new One Station Unit Training Course for MPs. I busted my butt, and my annual OER depicted my accomplishments: *"Captain Lindsey was specially picked for command because of her boundless energy, wide background, and complete devotion to the health, welfare, and morale of troops new in the army. She is definitely troop oriented. She is totally responsive and leads by example. She is straightforward, dependable, not afraid of challenges, a decisive self-starter, and a cool, efficient resource manager. She avidly supported and expanded team and individual sports and willingly contributed her gifted musical talent at post and community social activities. Maximum potential yet to be recognized. Recommend promotion and Command and General Staff College (C&GSC) ahead of contemporaries."*

Oh, how I wished the written words on an OER could become a reality. My potential level had changed from unlimited to maximum. After my seven-year break in service, I had proven that I had not lost my touch and was still operating on the same level as my OCS contemporaries who were now majors and LTCs. I was being recommended for promotion to the rank that I would have if I had not had a break in service. I was recommended for step 3, schooling at C&GSC, that prepared officers to become an LTC; but my cart was still way ahead of my horse. I had not completed MP Officer Advanced School. (step 2)—there was no way for me to put the horse ahead of the cart, unless God sent an angel to set things right.

I had to continue galloping ahead until the MPOA course was available in the next six months. I completed my assignment as a commander with another outstanding OER: *"Captain Lindsey has demonstrated singularly outstanding duty performance in all aspects of command. Articulate in both written and oral expression, she exhibits exceptional administrative talent. Most noteworthy is this officer's ability to communicate with senior and subordinates alike, eliciting respect, loyalty, dedication, and support. She is truly an outstanding officer, who should be considered for promotion, schooling, and positions of greater responsibilities ahead of her contemporaries."*

There it was again in the written word: "ahead of her contemporaries." My superiors kept telling the army that I should be placed ahead of my contemporaries and receive schooling that would prepare me for an LTC. But I had to proceed forward with my cart way ahead of the horse. I thanked God for the lack of strife during my time at the MP school, counted my blessings; and it became apparent that I had grown immensely in the past three years. Hallelujah, I was evolving and embracing the right spiritual and personal virtues. "You've blended into the white man's army and come a long way in your dreams of the Promised Land, Ms. Lee."

Despite being behind the power curve, I felt very good about my accomplishments. Upon my departure from command, I was presented with a Meritorious Service Medal to add to my Good Conduct and National Defense Medal. I was also behind in receiving awards (ribbons) for my outstanding performance; I never received my fair dues from WAC Center when I departed because of Lieutenant Colonel Brown. She would never think of recommending an award for me after I gave her so much grief. Oh, well, what's one little ribbon? *Success is not what you do, but how you feel about what you do!*

It was now time to go to step 2, even though I should be at step 3. After six months, I successfully completed the MPOA course and was ready to move on to another military journey as a certified MP officer. I received yet another outstanding rating from my faculty advisor upon completion of the course: *"Captain Lindsey is a highly motivated officer who has clearly exhibited the academic potential for attendance at the Command and General Staff College before her contemporaries. Her written project was without error, and her oral presentation clearly demonstrated that she is a truly professional briefer. Her leadership abilities are far above that of the average army captain . . . This officer demonstrates technical competence normally associated with field grade officers (major and above). Promote this officer ahead of her contemporaries and select for C&GSC."*

NOTE: I have included excerpts of my OERs throughout my book to depict what others described as my potential; however, the powers to be (white men, I am sure) at the Pentagon level obviously continued to ignore what the black military pen indicated for my future. Unfortunately, someone at the top level decided to make it impossible for me to achieve my rewards for performances well done during my military journey.

I completed step 2 and was once again told I should be at step 3 and promoted, but . . . So be it. Life went on in the slow lane as I prepared for my continuing quest. I had to be thankful for adapting well to the male-oriented environment without any evidence of struggling. *Was this all too good to be true? What was my destination now?*

CHAPTER 7

ROTC Foxhole

After completing my MP course in 1978, I requested an ROTC assignment at my alma mater so I could be home with my mother and daughter and pursue my master's degree. I felt that having an advanced degree may assist in getting promoted along with my contemporaries. It was a simple request because most of my classmates wanted MP assignments Stateside or overseas. Being an ROTC instructor was not challenging for a newly graduated MPOA officer, so I wasn't asking for much; but guess what? The ink on my last outstanding evaluation wasn't even dry yet before I noticed another ditch heading my way.

I received a call from my MP advisor in Washington DC, who was responsible for my assignments and career advancements. He told me that before I could have the job, I had to be interviewed by a white infantry colonel, who was in charge of the First Army ROTC regional headquarters located at Fort Bragg, North Carolina.

"Interviewed? Since when does an army officer have to be interviewed for an assignment?" I bluntly asked my advisor.

"Sorry, Lee. There's nothing we can do. Colonel Short is in charge of that ROTC region, and what he says, goes."

"Something doesn't sound right, Bill. What's the real deal behind all of this?"

He slowly responded. *"The bottom line is that Colonel Short thinks that you are too old for the job."*

"What? You've got to be kidding." I blurted out. *"Has he seen my OERs? Does he know my personal background?"*

"I tried my best to inform him, but he wouldn't listen."

"Bill, this isn't right. No one else in my class had hassles with their assignments."

I cringed as he remarked, *"I agree, but my boss said that you have to go to the interview."*

I angrily hung up the phone, as adverse thoughts flashed through my mind. *So this colonel thinks that at age thirty-six, I'm too old to cut the mustard on a college campus. He completely ignored my past outstanding officer evaluation reports. I had overcome racial and sexual inequities in the military, and I was now being slapped in the face with age discrimination. When will this stuff ever end?*

After I calmed down and resolved to *act my age,* I arranged to meet with Colonel Short (refraining from using his real name). Honey, I was fired up and ready to confront the man who had insulted my individuality and my age. I made the long drive to Fort Bragg, trying to maintain my composure despite the rage that ensued within. I arrived at the colonel's office donned in civilian attire rather than my uniform—a nonconformist, rebellious act on my part. The secretary announced my presence to Colonel Short, and I stood in front of his desk at the position of attention, saluted, and reported sharply to him.

He looked at me obviously wondering why I wasn't in uniform, returned my salute, and grunted, *"Have a seat, Captain Lindsey."*

Before he could continue speaking, I began my rehearsed dissertation. *"Sir, it appears that based on my age, you question my ability to perform this job. I had a seven-year break in service; therefore, my rank and age are inharmonious because of this event. I have outstanding OERs, a recommendation from the MP branch for this position; and I can do this job, despite your misconceptions about my age."*

"Captain, I have concerns about a thirty-six-year-old soldier establishing rapport with young college students. I feel a younger officer may be better for the job."

I leaned forward in my chair emphasizing, *"Colonel, I believe that if I were a thirty-six-year old, blond, blue-eyed, white male soldier, I would be sitting in my ROTC office instead of at your desk."*

He quickly interjected, *"That's not true. This has nothing to do with your race or your sex. I have concerns about your age and nothing else."*

"Age discrimination is just as offensive as racism or sexism! This is blatant prejudice on your part. Do I need to say more, Colonel?"

Colonel Short knew that I could cause him havoc if I decided to pursue this issue and file a discrimination charge against him with the army's inspector general's office. He leaned back in his chair and humbly remarked, *"Maybe I did jump the gun in your case. I see that you are a feisty officer who doesn't look her age. Let's try to reach a happy medium. You've got the job if Lieutenant Colonel Thomas, the professor of military science (PMS), agrees that he wants you at his college."*

I thought to myself, *"How white of you, Colonel. Passing the buck to another officer because you got your thing in a sling."* I looked directly into his eyes and said, *"I've already spoken to Lieutenant Colonel Thomas about my background and the job. He has no problems with my race, sex, or age and is anxiously awaiting my arrival, thank you."*

I sat back gently, crossed my arms and legs, awaiting his response.

Colonel Short cleared his throat and retorted, *"Well, if that's the case, you better get to your new assignment. We have nothing further to discuss, Captain."*

I briskly departed his office and Fort Bragg, feeling victory coupled with deep frustration. It is so demeaning when you have to *prove yourself* to another human being in the name of equality. ***Have the courage to stand your ground in fighting blatant injustices.***

A year later, I ran into Colonel Short at ROTC summer camp at Fort Bragg, approached him, and spoke to him jokingly. *"Hello, Colonel. Well, as you can see, this frail officer is still kicking. I'm sorry I wasn't what you thought I was."*

He looked at me with chagrin, saying, *"You've made your point very clear, Captain. I keep receiving reports of the outstanding rapport you have with the cadets. Keep up the good work."*

A pleasing chuckle churned within as I watched him friskily march away from me. Yes, I enjoyed this victory as I refused to be pushed into a ditch dug by someone who had misjudged me as a person and as a leader. *Thank you, dear Father, for your wisdom, guidance, and spiritual armor to outmaneuver another planned human sabotage.* Despite this triumph, I did not have the time to feel safe and secure from obstacles. A cloudy dust ball was brewing on my path as the ROTC job presented me with a bigger foxhole to conquer. Here I go again, ongoing strife in my everlasting Promised Land.

I walked directly into a lion's den occupied with combat-crazed white men, who were waiting to eat me alive. My immediate boss was Major Gray, a white infantry soldier whose father was a retired general. This in itself made the man a basket case because he was spinning his wheels in the army trying to live up to his father's image. The major made it perfectly clear that he thought there was no place for women in the army; therefore, this bigoted man and I immediately clashed.

"Major, I could care less what you think about women in the military. I've been in the army for eight years, and I'm here to stay. I would appreciate it if you would just let me do my job without having to deal with your bias."

"I'm your boss, and you can't talk to me like that, Captain," he shouted.

"I'm a person, and you can't treat me as if I'm a naive young female soldier. I will respect you, as long as I receive the same treatment."

From that initial confrontation, the ROTC foxhole began to spout its ugly head. This major was out to get me because I was not a *yes* person and had the nerve to speak my mind to him. Hell, I was older than this guy; and it was obvious that he had not interacted much with blacks, no less a black woman, so my bluntness only riled him more. To add to this dilemma, I had to work with two combat-oriented white male captains, who were also younger than me. When they caught a whiff of how Major Gray was going to treat me, they immediately got on his bandwagon. Lieutenant Colonel Thomas, the PMS, was the overseer of our extension ROTC program, but his office was located twenty-five miles away at a different university. I immediately alerted the PMS on the adverse treatment I received from Major Gray and his devoted followers.

"Captain Lindsey, I want you to hang in there and do your job. If the situation gets completely out of hand, you are to notify me immediately," instructed Lieutenant Colonel Thomas.

"Okay, I'll do my best, but I refuse to submit to the major's personal hang-ups and any dirty tactics. Sir, I will be in touch if it becomes unbearable."

I meditated and prayed for strength in combating my newest enemy—rulers of darkness and evil spirits in the positions of personally defined military power. But God is always with me during my times of strife, and a spiritual voice within spoke to me, *"Captain Lindsey, you're in the real army now. Christ's army! You will be doing battle the rest of your life, and the forces you will fight can only be defeated with spiritual weapons. Have complete faith in God and always don your spiritual armor in times of inequities."*

My military journey started taking a more defined spiritual path. With all the struggling in the past years, I relied upon God's wisdom and armed myself with his spiritually defined weapons: the belt of truth, the breastplate of righteousness, the shoes of peace, the helmet of salvation, the shield of faith, and the sword of spirit. I accepted the call to vigilance and to arms, knowing that God would be my protector and my strength. All I had to do was follow God's guidance and instructions. I must not get discouraged, give up, and continue doing what I know is right in God's eyes. I had to be of sober spirit and be on the alert, knowing that he would save me from my enemies. I charged ahead and embraced faith in God, as I dodged the fiery darts from my ROTC foes.

I started getting weary after a year when I discovered that I was doing most of the dirty work in the unit. I started off teaching freshman Military Science 100 classes and then directed to teach Military Science 400 to senior cadets. I was given additional duties as the recruiting officer, as the detachment administration officer, and as the scholarship program officer. My fellow male captains only had to be concerned with Military Science 200 and 300 classes—the macho combat-oriented courses that prepared cadets for ROTC summer camp evaluation.

Nevertheless, I hung in there, performed my duties in a professional manner, and tried to *be all that I could be* for the cadets. I was there to teach the students and prepare the seniors for active military duty; therefore, I had a dedicated mission to accomplish. By the end of my first year on the job and time for my annual rating, I was one tired puppy. Then the dirt hit the fan when Major Gray tried to end the year's battle with the stroke of his pen by giving me a derogatory OER.

Once again, a military person had the ultimate power to *make or break me* with the written words on an annual evaluation. I suddenly had visions of Lieutenant Colonel Brown dressed as a man in an army uniform. Again, I refused to accept or sign the OER. The ink was not dry on the OER before I found myself sitting at Lieutenant Colonel Thomas's desk. The situation was now very serious and I needed his help. For the past year, I kept notes in a little black book, which mainly covered questionable work ethics and professionalism on the part of all three officers. Major Gray even treated the cadets badly; he was a madman.

The rapport I established with the cadets was awesome, and I could depend upon them to come to the forefront if I needed them in my defense. I had performed my job over and beyond the call of duty. I was solely responsible for high student enrollment in the ROTC program, persuaded

females to pursue the course, and obtained numerous scholarships for the cadets. I took the initiative to form a proficient color guard and a drill team, which participated regularly in college and community events. My little black book contained ample ammunition on my male foes, and I had college and community support in opposing Major Gray's disparaging remarks.

Lieutenant Colonel Thomas was not pleased with the evaluation either. Unknown to me, the PMS wanted something tangible that he could use against Major Gray, who he also felt was somewhat deranged. Therefore, the information I provided him was fuel for his fire. Well, needless to say, the major's derogatory OER became a part of file 13, the wastebasket. He was reprimanded, and the PMS informed Major Gray that it was time for him to find a new home or resign from the army.

I also had some juicy stuff in my black book on the two captains. They were also reprimanded by the PMS and forced to change their evil ways, or their careers would be on the line. I did not have any more problems with these young men during the remainder of my assignment. In 2006, I was watching the news about the war in Iraq, and lo and behold, one of these ROTC officers is now a three-star general. I almost puked when I saw him, but I am sure he had no problems punching the right tickets to the top as a combat-oriented white man. I wish him the best.

God "don't like ugly" and his spiritual armor was smoking all over my body during this unnecessary battle. I stood my ground and refused to be intimidated by these evil white men. The ROTC foxhole closed, a new major was assigned, and I started my next year of ROTC on fresh, solid ground. However, I kept my spiritual armor close by just in case someone decided to attack. *Life is mothered by a conscious awareness of God: All else is experience.*

After three years, I successfully completed my ROTC assignment and received outstanding OERs and an Army Commendation Medal. With courage and complete faith in God, I overcame these man-made inequities, accomplished my mission with integrity and professionalism, and attained my masters degree in the process. My spiritual journey in this Promised Land continued as I prepared to ship out to another adventure in another country. *Please God, don't let me struggle any more!*

CHAPTER 8

Family Time and College

During the three years in my ROTC assignment, I was also struggling with family issues. I requested this assignment so I could be with my daughter, who was literally being raised by my mother. Chantay and my mother spent the summers with me when I was stationed in Alabama, but it was not the same as being with my child during her growing days. I had to sacrifice this role in order to take care of my family. My daughter was twelve years old when I returned home, and she was becoming rebellious to the point that my mother couldn't handle her. She was no longer that winsome chubby child and was developing into a blossoming beautiful, slim and trim adolescent searching for her identity. Chantay was very interested in modeling, so I permitted her to attend a Barbizon Modeling School. The school paid off  because it made Chantay more graceful, self-confident, and disciplined. Her tall, lanky body with a fresh complexion and flowing long hair made her a perfect candidate for modeling. The school assisted her in developing a portfolio that contained very professional pictures, and she was developing into a beautiful woman with unlimited modeling potential.

Since I was a musician, I was pleased that Chantay appeared to be interested in music and started playing the clarinet in the middle school band. I was excited about this, bought her a piano, and she began taking lessons. I wanted her to have the opportunities that I didn't have, but Chantay eventually lost interest in music. She dropped out of the band, and at age thirteen, she decided to become a majorette. This appealed more to her, complemented her modeling experience, and gave her more satisfaction than the band. She was a socialite, made friends easily, and seemed to be the leader of her peer groups.

My mother accepted my lifestyle from the first day I told her way back in the '70s. She always felt that I must do whatever made me happy. She met the majority of my gay friends and always welcomed them into her home. All she wanted was to see me happy and for Chantay to be raised properly. Every lesbian should have a mother like mine.

My goal was to get my masters degree, and this time, Chantay would be joining me on my next assignment. My mother would be relieved of her grandparent duties and have her home to enjoy in peace and quiet. Therefore, as I viewed it, the entire family had a mission. When Chantay turned fourteen, puberty kicked in like a wild horse. She was rebellious and seemed to be bored in our slow-moving, stifling-paced country town and her Redstone middle school environment. She started lashing out at her teachers, and one day she hit one of her male teachers.

"Mom, he called me a nigger, so I hit him," Chantay said in a very defensive tone.

I immediately went to the school for a conference with the teacher and the principal to try to resolve this issue. After getting feedback from Chantay's friends, other students, and teachers, there seemed to be some truth in what Chantay said really happened. The teacher she hit would not admit that he said anything derogatory, but I departed the school with the problem smoothed over without Chantay getting into serious trouble.

"You just can't go around punching out people when they upset you, Chantay."

"Mom, one thing I can't stand is to be called a nigger or a bitch. Those are fighting words for me, and I just can't help it," Chantay responded in a serious manner.

I had to chuckle under my breath because she was indeed her mother's daughter. I felt the same way and could also go off the deep end if someone called me those names. Then there was another incident when Chantay decided to try out *shoplifting* at one of the stores in the mall. She loved jewelry and took some earrings without paying for them; my naive daughter did not know that she was being watched by a store detective, who grabbed her as she left the store. Chantay was one scared puppy over this act, and she cried her heart out, fearing she was going to be sent to jail. We appeared before juvenile court, and she admitted her wrongdoing. The judge had her pay for the jewelry and put her on a couple of months' probation. After that, Ms. Chantay shaped up and changed her rebellious ways.

The big day at California State College finally arrived. As my name was called, I proudly walked across the stage to receive my masters of education degree in secondary guidance counseling and consulting. I still had six months before I would receive my next assignment; and regardless of where the army sent me, Chantay had to accompany me. I had to rescue her from the boredom of my small hometown and expose her to the real life in this Promised Land. I received my assignment, and lo and behold, it was to Germany. Deep down inside, I knew I would eventually have to go overseas, so I was not shocked. I announced to my family that I was going to be the deputy provost marshal at Hanau, MP station, and my reporting date was in September 1978. Out of nowhere, Chantay looked at me and blurted, *"I am not going to Germany."*

I gave her a devastating glare and commanded, *"Oh, yes, you are. You don't have any choice in the matter."*

My mother gave her a piece of her mind saying, *"That's right. You are going and that's that. I can't handle you anymore, and it's time for you to be with your mother."*

Chantay cried out, *"That's not fair."* I retorted, *"Life's not fair, my dear daughter."*

The case was closed, and Ms. Chantay had to prepare herself for a new adventure in the upcoming months. I viewed an assignment in Europe as a part of my journey and a challenge. I had survived the military for ten years and was halfway toward finishing my business with the army. Taking my daughter to a foreign country would do her good by giving her the opportunity to see what another part of the world is all about. This may be God's way of guiding me in order to help my daughter learn and grow. ***You'll never get to where you want to be, unless you let go of where you are now!***

I had many things to do in preparing for this assignment overseas: getting shots and passports, packing, shipping my car, finding a place to live, and enrolling Chantay in school. *What challenges lay ahead for my daughter and me?*

CHAPTER 9

Bound for Overseas Duty

Chantay and I arrived in Germany, and prior arrangements were made to stay at a guesthouse in Dieburg until I could find housing. Barbel and Hanz, the guesthouse owners, spoke English; were very friendly; and helped us get adapted to German life. We eventually became the very best of friends. I scuffled around getting Chantay registered in a DOD school, took an introductory German language course, studied and passed the German driving test, and settled in at my new job as deputy provost marshal (assistant police chief) in Hanau, ten miles from Dieburg.

I commuted to my new job and dropped Chantay off at her school located a mile from the army post. It didn't take Chantay long to adjust to school and European customs, and she started liking her new way of life. Housing on post was not available for us, so I found a place to stay off post. Chantay became actively involved in modeling, and Barbel helped us find places for her to *strut her walk*. As a beautiful tall, willowy black female, Chantay fit perfectly into the European environment. As usual, she was the leader of her peer group in school as well as socially. She learned to speak German well and became very independent. She used the bus and train to go to activities in Frankfurt

and Hanau and was flourishing by pursuing different outlets—skating, discos, modeling, and traveling to other countries. Barbel and Hanz fell in love with Chantay and exposed her to various local activities. My daughter was happy and adjusted very well, to the point that she did not have to worry about her race and began thinking and acting like a European.

Deep down inside, I knew that having Chantay with me was the best thing I could have done for her. She was maturing, and her rebellious adolescent stage seemed to dissipate. She was so attractive at age sixteen, and boys kept chasing after her. Since

53

I was a police officer on post, I set down the law that she would not date any soldiers. Chantay was obedient, made good grades in school, and was learning and growing in a foreign country. Within a year, she started dating an Italian boy from Naples who lived and worked in Frankfurt. Damiano was a very well-mannered, respectful, hardworking twenty-one-year-old, who fell deeply in love with Chantay. He had high aspirations, respected me and my daughter, and I liked him very much.

Chantay literally picked up the European ways and did not let the color of her skin get in her way. Discrimination was not evident in Germany, and we were treated as regular people. I saw a new person evolving in my daughter and felt very proud in the way she was adapting and handling life in general. Removing her from the stifling environment in my hometown was the best decision I could have ever made for her.

Barbel and I talked a lot about our individual lives; her husband was nothing more than a playboy, driving around in his big Mercedes, flashing money around as if he was rich. When I found out that he was cheating on my friend, Barbel, I really got upset and became very distant with him. Barbel knew all along that he had a mistress, but she somehow blocked it out. They had two sons, was more concerned about raising them and running her business. I felt so sorry for her and tried to be there for her whenever she was unable to deal with her hurt and pain. There was many a night that she and I sat at her bar, drinking cognac while she drowned in her tears because of this man.

One day I woke up moaning, *"Where am I?"*

As I tried to sit up in my bed, I felt an excruciating throb in my lower abdomen. I looked around and realized that I was lying in the intensive care unit in the military hospital in Frankfurt. I had just had a complete hysterectomy after years of complaining of pain during my menstrual cycle. Five years before I had tried to tell a doctor at Fort McClellan about my severe female problems, and he swore that it was merely psychological. Well, after being thoroughly checked by an army doctor in Germany, he discovered a cyst the size of an orange on my left ovary. *This did not originate in my mind!*

The doctor indicated that I could have my ovary removed and not have a complete hysterectomy saying, *"You may want to have more children, Captain Lindsey."*

"Doc, forget children. That's the last thing on my mind. I don't want to experience dysmenorrhea or have another period ever again in my lifetime. Take it all out, please," I exclaimed.

"Okay, if you say so," he responded. After my operation, Barbel insisted that I stay at her guesthouse to recuperate; I accepted. Barbel was happy to have me at her place, and it didn't take long for me to heal. It was time to be promoted to major and assume

more responsibilities. After a year and a half at Hanau, I was assigned a new job in Frankfurt at V Corps headquarters. I received two OERs during my tenure at Hanau and had done very well without any serious disruptions. I also received a special OER for serving as the acting provost marshal for three months right before I departed for my new assignment. My two bosses, a major and an LTC, both shipped out at the

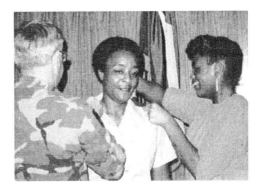

same time, leaving me on my own and in charge until replacements arrived. I simply accepted it as a challenge and did my thing, using all my spiritual virtues to ensure I did not fail. ***Do what feels right!***

I was rated by the colonel and the general in charge of the Hanau installation. The colonel wrote: *"Captain Lindsey has earned this special OER for a remarkable series of accomplishments during a short, very trying period when an inexcusable breakdown in the personnel management system prevented the PMO LTC slot to be filled. In fact, Captain Lindsey was the only officer in the PMO during the entire period. She didn't just 'hold on,' but also exercised outstanding maturity, coolness, and leadership in supervising and managing all divisions of PMO.*

"She attacked and solved some long-standing and nagging problems, implemented and later updated a crime prevention program, significantly improved the atmosphere and cooperative climate among commanders, Criminal Investigations Division (CID), MP Customs, and Military Intelligence Agencies, and reinforced U.S./German police cooperation by establishing joint patrols and mutually supporting radar enforcement in the community. The procurement of word processing within the PMO under her direction was the capstone to an absolutely superb performance by a singularly outstanding officer. Promote now. She has proven with certainty her ability to command at the 05 (LTC) level."

The general's comments included, *"Captain Lindsey's performance has been singularly outstanding and shows beyond any doubt that her potential to successfully handle very responsible positions ranks with those who are rated one out of one hundred. She is clearly the best MP captain I have known and is one of the best company grade officers of any branch I have known. She is ready for promotion and increased responsibility now."*

Oh, how I wished the written word could become a reality. I was praised for performing at the level I was destined to be before my break in service, yet there was no way I could be assured of making LTC. I still had not been selected for C&GSC that would permit me to make LTC. I eventually discovered that my age was now an issue and that younger officers were being picked up for the school. Even one of my platoon officers that worked for me when I was a WAC company commander got chosen for school before me. I was being passed over because I was forty-one years old. I tried taking the C&GSC correspondence course as a possible buffer, but I had too many irons in the fire (work, music, softball, and Chantay) to be successful at completing and passing this course. As I look back, I guess I should have rearranged my priorities. I truly felt that the system would bypass me anyway based on my age; there simply was no way for me to play catch-up with my contemporaries. I had gone the complete gamut of discrimination: sex, race, and now age. *When would it ever end?*

I managed to survive my Hanau assignment without tripping into a valley. Well, I take that back. I did have a little ditch to face based on the actions of my beloved daughter. One day Chantay got involved in a confrontation with a girl who happened to be the daughter of my immediate boss. The colonel's twenty-two-year-old daughter and Chantay, who was sixteen at the time, got into a fight in the housing complex in Hanau. I was contacted at home by one of my sergeants, who told me about the incident. I went looking for Chantay in the housing area where the incident occurred, but I couldn't find her. I kept searching the area and finally decided to go to the skating rink downtown to see if she was there. Sure enough, she was skating like nothing had happened. When she saw me, she approached me with a serious look on her face.

"Okay. Tell me what happened," I said calmly.

"Mom, the girl kept messing with me and called me a bitch. She was trying to show off in front of people in the housing area by agitating me. So I took off my high-heeled shoe and whipped her butt," Chantay remarked casually.

Dear God, why did you have to make my daughter so much like me? When will my child learn to use tact and diplomacy, rather than her fists in settling disputes? Oh, well. I guess I'll have to face the music with my boss when I go to work.

I didn't wait to be called into the office by my boss. I showed up at his door early the next morning, ready to discuss what had happened between our kids.

"Captain Lindsey, my daughter was just as much to blame as yours. Girls will be girls. I told my daughter that she was too old to be hanging around teenagers," he said as if in an apologetic mode.

"I'm sorry this all happened. My daughter is quick to start swinging when someone calls her a derogatory name."

"I understand. As far as I'm concerned, it's over. Don't worry about it."

I was expecting the worst but left his office feeling completely relieved. Chantay was well-known on post including the people I worked for and those who worked for me. She was normally a good kid who socialized well with all ages. She and I were often invited to the colonel's house; after this incident, all contact with the colonel's family came to an abrupt end.

I had successfully made it through my first overseas assignment without facing devastating obstacles, and my military journey seemed to be on a very smooth track. Chantay was happy, and I was ready for a new job. Okay, was this all too good to be true?

CHAPTER 10

My Guardian Angel in Europe

I was promoted to major and headed to my new job in Frankfurt at the V Corps Provost Marshal's office. I was assigned as the PMO operations officer which entailed being the advisor to the deputy provost marshal on all law enforcement and physical security activities within the corps—a major tactical headquarters in the Federal Republic of Germany. I assisted in the formulation of policies for ten provost marshal offices throughout Germany, and I also supervised the operations section to ensure that all MP reports were provided daily to the V Corps two-star commanding general.

During this time frame, bomb threats to U.S. military personnel and housing areas were on the increase in Europe. Antiterrorism was a major concern at V Corps because people were literally being killed by terrorists. Our office worked closely with the German Polizei in fighting terrorism; I learned a lot by working with them and got a bird's-eye view of how things operate at higher levels. My bosses, a LTC and a colonel, had complete confidence in me and regularly sent me to brief the general and his staff on MP matters.

I found military housing for us in Frankfurt, and Chantay was doing very well. She was now a senior in DOD Frankfurt high school, which was located next to the V Corps headquarters. She and Damiano were still dating, and he wanted to marry her; but Chantay wasn't ready for marriage. She was a very independent, self-reliant teenager who enjoyed doing her thing. She traveled everywhere on school projects and leisurely pursuits. I could get travel rates for her at a cheaper rate, and she was anxious to see the world: Spain, Switzerland, Belgium, Holland, Italy, and France. My daughter was exposed to the world, and it was the best experience I could have ever wanted for her. I also traveled a lot during my tour in Europe as a result of my job, music, softball, and on a leisurely basis.

I even got my mother to visit me for a month so I could expose her to another country. A dear hometown friend was kind enough to make the arrangements and flew with my mother to Germany. We had a good time, traveling throughout Europe; and I took my mother to Paris, the Black Forest, Brussels, Amsterdam, and a boat ride down the river Rhine. She also enjoyed watching

my softball games and listening to me play music. My mother truly enjoyed herself, and she blended in well with my German and military friends, who treated her so kindly. She had an experience that she could always cherish.

Everything started out great in my new assignment in Frankfurt, and I had very good bosses who were concerned for my welfare and taught me well. My immediate boss was a black LTC, who had been through a series of trials and tribulations in the military that would prevent him from ever making colonel. He was very empathetic with my constant struggles with discrimination and tried to encourage me to make the best of situations that I had no control over. He was a proud, professional man, and we became very good friends. My second boss was a terrific white colonel, who would not harm a fly. He played by the military rules, did everything the right way; he treated everybody with kindness and stood up for them whenever necessary. So I was surrounded by angels that guarded over me and taught me the tricks of the MP trade; it was a serious and dangerous time in Europe with terrorism on the forefront.

Within months, I was selected for a special duty assignment for fifty days in Great Britain as the protocol officer (public relations) for the task force commander during a joint forces special operation. My job was to coordinate staff assistant duties between the United States, NATO commands, and several foreign countries; it would prove to be a very different and rewarding experience. I did not particularly care much for England with its bland food and conservative lifestyle, but I found a way to enjoy myself in London. My job kept me stuck out in the woods with special forces soldiers and other military personnel from foreign countries, and I managed to meet some very interesting people. A senior officer from Greece wanted to marry me and go off with him into his Grecian sunset, but I had to say no. He was an interesting gentleman.

I greeted, orientated, and made everyone feel comfortable as they played their simulated war games. Believe it or not, I ran into one of my ROTC cadets from Pennsylvania while playing in the fields of England; he was a special forces soldier, who had progressed well in the army. We were so happy to see each other, and we almost broke out in tears. I felt like a proud mother when he told me about his successful military pursuits. We sat around and chatted about our days back at ROTC, laughed about the crazy major and two captains, and talked about his experiences in the army. He was very conscientious, professional, and dedicated. Seeing him unexpectedly in a foreign country was a marvelous event, and it made me feel so good inside to see his progress.

I completed my special job in England and received a very nice report written by the task force commander: *"Major Lindsey, an outstanding officer, was exceptionally conscientious and devoted toward mission accomplishment. She worked extremely hard in planning, developing, coordinating, and supervising an effective visitor program for Joint Combined Readiness Exercise FLINTLOCK, which was conducted in the United Kingdom and involved twelve other countries from the Arctic Circle to North Africa. Her meticulous attention to detail and sense of responsibility resulted in an unusually substantial amount of praise from all exercise visitors.*

"She effectively and efficiently worked with representatives from the various branches of the United States and Allied National Services. Without question, she demonstrated the ability to handle diverse and stressful requirements with ease and total professionalism. Major Lindsey is an absolutely superb officer: bright, loyal, versatile, and totally dedicated. She developed, coordinated, and executed the most successful FLINTLOCK series visitor program I have witnessed. Select her for advanced schooling and challenging assignments, which will broaden her experiences and capitalize on demonstrated potential."

I felt good after this job well done in a foreign country, which gave me a rewarding military experience in the all-man army. I had regained my faith in mankind and was feeling successful in all I did.

Just as my overseas assignment was coming to an end, Chantay decided to flaunt her independence and freedom by telling me that she was not returning to the States with me. She wanted to remain in Germany, find a job, and live with Damiano until she decided when she was going to marry him. My mother freaked and kept telling me that I should not leave Chantay to fend for herself in a foreign country. After deep meditation and prayer, I decided that my daughter was now an adult, had matured these past three years, and I would support her decision. I needed to sever the umbilical cord and let her live her life her way. I was not going to dictate what she should or should not do. I had a heart-to-heart talk with Damiano about the proper treatment of my daughter, which was not a problem for him; he truly loved Chantay, would care for her, and wanted to marry her as soon as possible. So I would be leaving my daughter in Germany when I departed for my next assignment Stateside.

However, my overseas tour was not about to end so successfully. Wouldn't you know that when I thought I had succeeded without struggling, the demon jumped into my path presenting me with a serious obstacle!

My two favorite MP bosses were due to ship out a few months before me. I received an outstanding OER from them and truly enjoyed working for and with these fine male officers. I really hated to see them leave me. I had three months to go before I shipped out, new bosses were reassigned, and I had to readapt to their ways during this short period. One would think all would go smoothly, but my luck was such that a *ditch* readily appeared in my path upon the arrival of my new superiors.

My good, caring, angelic bosses walked out of my life, only to be replaced by the bad, wicked guys. One of the white LTCs who worked in the same office was still on board, and he was a *yes-man,* who tried to get ahead by kissing butt. He didn't like me much because I was a go-getter, and he saw how my superiors treated me with kindness and respect. He immediately catered to the new colonel's wishes. I was left alone to defend myself from another lion's cage occupied by a colonel, a LTC, and a black Uncle Tom major. These guys came in with a new game plan, which included changing everything in the PMO.

Oh, Lord, please be with me during this short period. I decided to stay calm and cool and laid back, attempting to stay out of their way. There wasn't much for me to do in three months, so this should have been an easy feat. But these guys were devils from Hades. The colonel was a crazed soldier just like the major I encountered at ROTC; he felt there was no place for women in the army and was bent on impressing the V Corps Commanding General and his staff about his competency as an MP. The white LTC joined in and kissed butt to please the colonel's philosophy especially if it meant ostracizing me. The black major, who was married to a white army nurse, was so passive and pitiful, that I couldn't stand being in his presence. He was nothing more than a brownnoser black man that made me nauseous. When he saw that I would not have anything to do with him, he joined the lion's den with the other worthless male creatures.

Well, I was tired and fed up with a constant thorn in my side about women in the military. This shit was getting old. But I decided to leave my fighting armor in its case and decided not to participate in any battle. I opted to lie low, thinking all would be well in the few months I had left. So I went against the most important lessons I had learned in the past—be alert, stand my ground, don my spiritual armor, and prepare for a fight. Instead, I retreated and tried to avoid conflict for the next three months. *Did it work? Hell, no!*

By retreating, lying low, and trying to stay out of the enemy's way, I was on the defensive rather than the offensive. I was so involved in protecting myself that I did not pay close attention to what I did. Lo and behold, I made a big mistake by doing something innocent, but stupid. I was in the process of preparing to ship my household goods back to the States. I had to turn in my full issue of field training equipment (gas mask, poncho, tent gear, etc.). All of this gear was stored in a consolidated area for our MP unit. I was not paying attention to what I was doing, and in my rush to pack and ship out, I accidentally took another soldier's gear and turned it into the supply issue point. It never occurred to me that I had done something so dumb.

Before I could rectify the mistake, the soldier reported a theft of his equipment. It was then that I realized that in my rush, I had inadvertently taken his gear. My field equipment had been packed up with my household goods and was on its way back to the States. I tried to explain to the big bad colonel what happened, and suddenly I saw a special gleam in his eye. He was not going to let this one pass. I knew that I was down for the count and braced for the worst. He decided to make a big issue out of this event and immediately started digging a trench just for me. He had his *butt-kissing LTC* begin a CID investigation into the situation, even though I had already told him what happened. Well, he insisted upon proceeding, with his priority being to make an example out of me and what MPs should and should not do. The LTC and the major took off running with this case, anxiously trying to discredit me as an officer and a female.

The CID commander, who I worked closely with in the past and knew very well, even turned on me. He was planning to start an in-depth investigation, as if I had committed burglary or robbery. I was defenseless and found myself hanging out on a limb all by myself as these men kept digging the trench deeper, so they could shoot me down into what was now becoming a big crevice. I had to blame myself for this hole that was being dug with a big sign with my name on it. I had been off guard and inattentive in my efforts to retreat from my foes. *I messed up, but I was not a thief. Now what?*

Thank God, my good name and various performance was well-known by the V Corps commander, who was a humane black Christian male two-star general. I spent many a day briefing him on MP activities, and I presented him with several softball trophies for first place team wins. I also performed with my jazz band at community and post functions that he hosted. He knew me as a person and a professional soldier,

To Lee, with respect and best wishes

and I admired and respected him to the utmost. He was a spiritual man with pure understanding and keen wisdom; and when he got wind of what was going on in the PMO, he jumped right in to get all the facts surrounding my case.

He eventually called me into his office to get my side of the story, and he was very attentive and compassionate. I told him exactly what happened from trying to avoid conflict from these men by staying out of their way as they made MP changes. I admitted that I had messed up by not paying attention to what I was doing while hurriedly trying to ship out to my next assignment.

Major General Curry was a spiritual, no-nonsense person, and he related to me in that fashion. We discussed my trials and tribulations as a black female, MP officer of age, and my nonselection to C&GSC with no hopes of making LTC. He shared some of his struggles in the military with me in his rise as one of the few black two-star generals. Ironically, General Curry was born, raised, and graduated from a small town thirty miles from my hometown. He told me that he overcame his military struggles by having complete faith in God and that it worked. We continued talking about God and the need for constant spiritual inspiration in our lives in order to make it in this complex world—what I refer to as my Promised Land. It was the most inspiring and uplifting conversation that I ever had during my time in the military. No one ever approached me on the spiritual level before, which was a new and rewarding experience for me.

"*Okay, Major. You messed up. I am now officially giving you a verbal reprimand for your mistake. I want you to make arrangements to pay for the field gear before you ship out.*"

"*Yes, sir,*" I responded meekly.

"*I want you to be cautious and alert at all times in the future to avoid being snarled into another lion's den. I have had concerns about the new leadership in the provost marshal's office, and I want your input. Tell me what's really happening in that office,*" he said in an authoritative manner.

I proceeded to give my professional perspective of what I observed going on in the PMO that appeared to be a very unhealthy setting. He listened attentively as I told him my perceptions. When I was finished, he thanked me for my feedback.

As I prepared to leave his office, the general stood up and said, "*I want to thank you for the services you rendered to the community in your job, on the softball field, and with your music. You are a very talented, service-minded person, and I wish you the best of luck in all your endeavors. I pray that God will be with you always.*"

He then reached into his desk drawer, pulled out a small plaque, and wrote something on the back of it. He gave me the plaque saying, "*Keep this as a reminder when you think things are really getting tough.*"

I took the plaque and read it: "*Lord, help me to remember that nothing is going to happen to me today that you and I together can't handle.*"

I turned the plaque over to see what he had written. It read, "*Frankfurt, Germany, 11 Sept. 1984 . . . To Lee, with great respect,*" signed Major General J. R. Curry.

Tears came to my eyes as I thanked him for the inspirational plaque. He then approached me with his six-foot-six body and gave me a big bear hug saying, "*Good luck to you in your next assignment. If you need me, call any time.*"

He gave me a card where he could be reached when he returned Stateside; I believe that he was thinking about retiring. That blessed, angelic man made my day—made my European assignment meaningful. *God is love. God is good.*

When I returned to my office, everyone looked at me, wondering what the general had said to me during my visit. I ignored them all and began packing up my desk items. I did not share any information with anyone as to what had occurred in the general's office. I made arrangements to pay $300 for the field gear equipment and began preparing for my departure from V Corps.

I received word from one of my enlisted friends in the PMO that the general laid down the law in the office. He said, "*The general told everyone that your case was over and to 'cease and desist' on pursuing it any further. He also implied that some professional changes need to be implemented with the MP staff and informed the colonel that the sooner he got started, the better. The general jumped into the colonel's britches, big-time.*"

My friend chuckled as he related this particular gossip to me saying, "*You know, Major Lindsey, the colonel, the LTC, and the major think that you've been sleeping with the general; and that's why he forced them to get off your case.*"

I howled when he told me this and said, *"If they only knew, Sergeant. Thanks for the information. Man, I would have loved to have seen their faces when the general confronted them.*

I relished the thought of the devils in the lion's cage being brought to their knees. I had to laugh to myself on my friend's comments about the general and me being involved. *A spiritual lesbian and a wise Christian man having a lustful affair—I don't think so.* I knew that these men did not like the rapport that I had with the general. It didn't help any by having a picture of me and the general on my desk in which we were clasping each other, arm in arm, as we posed for a softball photograph. Before they arrived, I had been hard at work doing a professional job, establishing respect from my superiors in the process. These military men were jealous of me and only wanted to defeat me. But I was a harmless black woman, who was respected and treated fairly by past bosses and an angelic general who was wise enough to get to the truth. I had learned another worthwhile lesson, while avoiding a well-laid trench that was meant to engulf me. ***Pay attention to what you are doing at all times!***

I packed up, ready to leave Germany and return to the States to my new assignment. I reflected during my flight back to States and realized that each valley experience was nothing more than a blessing for me. I was growing spiritually and gaining strength and wisdom in the eyes of the Lord. Everything happens for a reason or a season, and I was indeed having my share of happenings.

The three years overseas were the most rewarding experiences in my life. My family and I got to see places that one only gets to view in books or on TV. I resolved issues involving my daughter, as I witnessed her grow and evolve into a very strong, proud, self-reliant black woman. I recalled her strutting across the platform at Frankfurt High School as she received her diploma. Three years before, she was a rebellious young kid stuck in a rut, screaming for adventure and freedom in search of her identity. Now I saw my daughter as a fine, beautiful, courageously tenacious young woman, who had become very self-sufficient and more confident.

Yes, Mother, we did well. God was with us and truly guided us in raising Chantay. I was not troubled with leaving Chantay in Germany because I knew that my daughter was a survivor and that all would work out well for her and for the best. I had faith that God would watch over her as usual.

My mind kept reflecting as the plane soared back to U.S. soil. I had met so many different people from different countries and made so many friends in Europe. Barbel was so sad to see me leave. We had some good times together, and I knew that she loved me deeply. She kept telling me that she was going to come to the United States and open up her own restaurant. She promised me that she would find a way to leave her husband and find happiness. I could still see the sad look on her face as I said my good-byes to her.

Five years after I departed Germany, Barbel contacted me to tell me the good news. She got rid of Hanz and found a nice American, Mike, who supervised a commissary in Germany. He treated her like a queen; they eventually got married, had a son; and Barbel is living happily with her new family in Hanover. God is indeed good! We managed to keep in touch and talked with each other by phone during Christmastime.

In 2005, I met my dear friend, Barbel; her husband; and son in Harrisburg. Mike's parents live there, and they were in the States traveling, called me; and we got together for a weekend of reminiscing and fun, fun, fun. Barbel even brought me a big bottle of Asbach from Germany. It was great to reunite with my loving German friend. One day I hope to return to Germany and spend quality time with her.

As I continued with my memories of Germany, I recalled the many accolades and written praises I received for performances well executed. As a result of my conflict with the devils from hell, I was once again cheated out of a noteworthy, earned ribbon for meritorious service or an Army Commendation Medal. Sounds like the good old days with my female pal, Lieutenant Colonel Brown. But who's to say what constitutes a reward? I learned new jobs, attacked new challenges, and achieved everything I did in the workplace, and continued doing the loves of my life: playing music and softball. Who could ask for anything more? I was blessed.

Despite what my past exemplary performances as a soldier clearly dictated where I should be in the rank structure, I could no longer dwell on the built-in inequities that I had no control over. There was no way that I would realistically be selected for attendance at the school I needed in order to be promoted to LTC. I accepted it and had to let go of the dream of attaining my fair share. *So had I failed?*

No, and it is quite the opposite. My success would never be determined by what I received—ribbons, medals, good OERs, correct schooling, promotions and a pat on the back, a trophy, or a plaque. My success would always be a result of how I feel about what I do. So I would no longer pine, whine, or complain about the obstacles that prevented me from any further upward mobility in the army. I did my best with integrity, and my final rewards are not to be of this world.

I have five more years to serve in the army before I will attain the goal that I set in 1974: retirement. I overcame many a valley and learned some very important lessons these past ten years. So I departed Germany, embracing all the good times, all the wonderful and positive experiences, and thanked God for the worthwhile lessons he showed me during my travels. It is now time to return home to the Promised Land and continue on my spiritual military journey. The next five years should be a breeze for me. *Well, let's see if this is true.*

Everything I experience is God's way to help me discover who I am!

CHAPTER 11

A Fiasco at Aberdeen Proving Grounds

Well, I was back on U.S. soil—the home of the brave and free, the land of the American dream, baseball, apple pie, and good old outright discrimination. *How is it that I could go overseas and be treated like a real person of worth only to return to the United States to face another big valley of injustice? Yeah, believe it or not, it was happening again.* I excitedly reported to my new duty station in Maryland, where I was assigned as the new provost marshal at Aberdeen Proving Grounds. I was ready to be the chief of police and do the best that I could do, when all of a sudden I found myself in the midst of another struggling journey.

This time my boss-to-be was a white two-star general, who decided that he wanted a LTC for his provost marshal instead of a major. *Here I go again; when would it ever end?* Now this general had access to my records and what I had done in the military for the past ten years. The MP branch recommended me for the job based on my outstanding past performance. *Yes, I had walked on water with combat boots for the past six years. I wasn't an LTC, and it was obvious that I would never become one; so what was this white man's problem?* I was back to my old self after my last call to battle. There would be no retreating this time, and I was ready and dug myself deep in my trench, fired up, wearing my full spiritual armor. I started my offensive tactics by refusing to sign in at the post, which could automatically lock me into remaining there. For thirty days, I was unassigned to a military post, while I battled fiercely against this man-made injustice.

During my first week on post, I couldn't deal with the general personally because he was somewhere overseas; and I had to wait for his return. His bosses tried to keep me calm in the interim and tried to explain what the general's rationale was for not wanting me as his provost marshal. To add to the dilemma, the general had also upset a black male LTC, who was the physical security officer for the installation. The general's plan was to put me in the physical security slot and move the LTC to my slot. Well, the LTC didn't want the job and was quite comfortable where he was. And of course, I wasn't budging because it was not right, not ethical, and downright discriminatory. So I wasn't accepting anything anyone had to say to me about the general's rationale.

The chief of staff was a black male colonel and the number 3 man in charge. This man tried to convince me that I needed to do what the general had decided and not fight it. *Oh no, Mr. Yes-man, you got the wrong gal.* He and I parted company very quickly. There was nothing this colonel could do to assist me in my battle except trip me right into the general's man-made stupid trench. I immediately called the MP branch and complained to them about my dilemma. They tried to convince me to sign in, and I refused outright to do any such thing. I told them I was tired of being treated like this when I reported in for a new assignment and reminded them of my ROTC initiation. Enough is enough.

The MP branch tried to calm me down and said they would start looking for another post for me to go to. I told them point-blank that I was not leaving Maryland, so don't even think about another state. I already had a house in Germantown to live in, and it would be a four-hour drive to visit my mother in Pennsylvania. Well, the general was away longer than everyone expected, so I kept building my case in his absence. I had to remain on post and live in a hotel room for thirty days. I called my one and only mentor, Brigadier General Sherian Cadoria, the same black female officer who had helped me get back on active duty ten years before. She was stationed at the Pentagon and was now a one-star  general. Our paths crossed while we were both stationed in Germany, and she was one hardworking, professional soldier. I had the deepest respect for her, not only as a friend, but also for her ability to overcome the inequities I know she faced as a black female; yet she managed to attain the rank of general. It had to be a hard road for her to travel, but I know her spirituality and faith got her through many a valley. I told her about my situation, and she immediately said she would look into it and told me to merely be cool and not do anything.

While waiting for guidance from my friend and the MP branch, I snooped around and gathered information about what was going on postwide as well as in the provost marshal office (PMO). I would be replacing a male white major who was retiring and had not faired well in his job. So he had to go. Maybe this was why the general didn't want a major. But this guy's ineffectiveness had nothing to do with me. This had to do with principle, and I wasn't giving up without a good fight. The PMO was in a disaster with no defined leadership, and the soldiers were simply doing their thing. Crime and traffic violations were rampant on post. Once the MPs at the PMO office got to know me, they wanted me to stay, fight my cause, and take over the job. They started getting upset over the general's decision to move me elsewhere and tried providing me with moral support.

I also discovered that other units were in disarray with lack of leadership and direction. The big shots at the command level were scared to death of the general and didn't particularly seem to like their jobs either. This installation was nothing more than a can of worms, and it sounded like the two-star general was not playing with a full deck of cards.

Rumors began to spread around the post about this black female major who was creating havoc, and the personnel people didn't know what to do; I still refused to sign in. I patiently waited for word from the Pentagon and tried to stay out of trouble. Since I had no place to work in, I decided to drive to other military posts in the immediate area and check out their situations. I stopped in at the PMO office at Fort Meade and talked to the colonel in charge. I told him what was happening with me at Aberdeen, and he was sympathetic and a really nice guy. Unfortunately he didn't have an opening in his office; and after spending hours with him, he said he would snatch me up in a minute if he had someplace to put me. I ran into this same colonel five years later. He was retired and working for a law enforcement agency in Atlanta. When I contacted him after I retired and moved to Atlanta, he tried to convince me to come to work for him as a police officer with the Georgia Bureau of Investigation. So there were still some good guys around in my Promised Land. This helped me to keep my faith in mankind, which was beginning to be harder and harder to do lately.

I departed from Fort Meade and checked out a small post located at Frederick, Maryland—Fort Detrick. It was a medical research and development installation with a small provost marshal's office that had civilian DOD police instead of military police personnel. I went to see the post commander, who turned out to be a fantastic, compassionate colonel with a great sense of humor and an unbelievable drive. Colonel Hoke was obviously a very good commander and very people oriented. I told him my story, and he became extremely interested. He informed me that he had a young white female captain as his provost marshal and that her performance was very poor. She was immature, gullible, and inexperienced to the point of being sexually involved with soldiers on post. Colonel Hoke was not pleased with her at all. His PMO office slot was for a captain, and it was a small closed post with not much crime or traffic problems. Their biggest problem was maintaining adequate physical security for all the buildings on post that housed highly sensitive and infectious materials (biological and chemical warfare).

The colonel and I hit it off well, and he immediately started plotting. The young captain was due to ship out in a few months, and he suggested that I contact my branch and alert them that he wanted me for her replacement. This meant I would be accepting a job inconsistent with my rank, but I knew that I was not going to work for the two-star madman that I hadn't even met yet. There were no other military posts in the immediate area except DC at the Pentagon or the Hoffman Building, and I wasn't really ready for that chaotic environment. So at least I had an ace in the hole with Fort Detrick whenever I faced the general. I thanked the colonel and headed back to my battleground at Aberdeen.

The general finally returned to his office, and I was immediately instructed to report to him ASAP. I took my good old time getting there to the point of walking from my hotel room to his office at the headquarters. I was fully donned in my six-piece spiritual-armor gear, ready to confront my enemy face-to-face. The first thing the general did wrong was to talk to me alone without witnesses. I reported to him with my snappy military salute.

"Have a seat, Major Lindsey. Now tell me why you've refused to sign in."

"Well, sir, it's like this. Once I heard that you had plans to put me into a slot other than as the provost marshal, I did not think signing in would be the wise thing to do. I wanted to wait and discuss the matter with you."

"Well, Major, the provost marshal's job is a very important position with huge responsibilities. I prefer to have an LTC in that position. I want you to take the physical security job so I can move the LTC to the PM job."

I pulled out the old cliché that I had used on the infantry colonel at Fort Bragg: *"Now, sir, I'm sure if I were a blue-eyed, blond, white male major, I would be sitting at my PM desk working right this minute. I have just returned from a three-year tour in Germany as a deputy provost marshal, an acting provost marshal (PM), an MP operations officer, and a physical security officer. My branch recommended me for a PM position based on my demonstrated abilities, which my OERs support to the utmost. Yet I hear you saying that I'm not good enough for the job as PM on your post. I came from V Corps where I had to deal with terrorism, bombings, and killings on military installations, and you have the nerve to infer that your post has more responsibilities than what I faced in Germany?"*

He angrily interjected and bluntly said, *"What you did in Germany has nothing to do with my post. I've got a nuclear reactor plant here that is crucial to my operation and must be protected. The PM job is very important, and I have serious crime and drug problems. I want you to be the physical security officer and that's that."*

"Well, General, that's not acceptable for me. I requested a PM job, not a physical security job. I did my physical security stint at V Corps, and I'm not doing it here. Let's get to the bottom line, General. The truth is that you don't want two black female officers in charge of the PMO, even though your lily white male major could not cut the mustard. You could care less about what my records say I can or cannot do. You keep harping that you want an LTC to take over. You haven't even checked my records, my age, my background—nothing. You just made a decision based on your personal hang-ups on race, sex, rank, and who knows what else. That equates to discrimination, General."

He tried to interject, but I continued in a forceful manner. *"Plus the LTC doesn't want to be provost marshal, so you're trying to screw up two officers based on your personal desires."*

He jumped up out of his chair, looked at me, and stuck his finger out at me saying, *"Major, get the hell out of my office."*

I got up out of my chair, briskly walked out of his office, and slammed the door behind me. The black chief of staff looked strangely at me as I strutted down the hallway. He said nothing, and I ignored him completely. I was one angry soldier; but I was glad the general and I were one-on-one, so I could openly relate what I had to say. After all, no one is supposed to talk to a two-star general in the manner that I did. *Hey, he's a man and not a god that we, lowlife subordinates, have to do whatever he dictates—not this lady. I refuse to conform to these silly military myths. Hell, he's just a man who thinks those two stars pinned on his shoulders give him power over everyone.* And he had his staff jumping around like dogs trying to obey him.

I learned my lesson: I can and will stand up and fight any injustice placed before me. So be it. I walked slowly back to my hotel room, reflecting on what had just transpired between the madman and me. I really pissed off this general, and he was fuming. But he also pissed me off, and I was fuming. The walk helped calm me down, and I knew there was no way I could remain on the installation. I had to think about using my ace in the hole. I called the MP branch, alerted them about the clash with the general, and told them to get me off this post now. I informed them about my chat with the commander at Fort Detrick and the offered assignment. They said they would give him a call.

Eventually General Cadoria called me from the Pentagon and told me that I had a blatant case of discrimination. She had conferred with the inspector general (IG) located at the Pentagon, and they informed her that the general was way off base with his decision. I told her about my confrontation with the general and that he was a downright madman, unwilling to budge; and it was time for me to get off this post. I also told her I had found a place to work if the MP branch would agree to arrange the assignment. She said she had other things she wanted to check out and that she would get back to me. I thanked her and hung up, feeling more at peace.

I hung around the PMO for a while, ventilated some with the troops, and eventually went to my room. The next morning I received word from the MP branch, who said that they could arrange for me to take the assignment at Fort Detrick. I could work as a project officer for the next couple of months until the young captain shipped out. I said fine and thanked them. I know that General Cadoria must have contacted them; that was some fast work. That afternoon, I was told to report to the general's office ASAP. It was time to face the final lap of my battle. I adjusted my spiritual armor, ready to charge ahead, and went off to see my favorite guy, the madman from hell.

I arrived at headquarters and was instructed to report to the general. *Now dig this: I opened the door, walked to the general's desk, sharply saluted, and stood at parade rest in front of him. Lo and behold, the room was filled with three other officers: the general's executive officer, the chief of staff, and some other colonel I didn't know. Hey, the general was prepared for me this time, wasn't he?* I sharply stood in front of the general's desk at parade rest as he spoke.

"Major, I see you've been very busy. Looks like you've contacted everyone you know in the Pentagon."

I didn't say a word and simply stood rigidly in front of him waiting to hear what more he had to say. He continued once he realized that he was not going to get a response from me.

"Anyway, I've reviewed your case and decided that you can have the PM position as long as you realize the responsibilities it involves and do your job."

Well, in the back of my mind, I interpreted this to mean that I could have the job; but if I screwed up, my butt belongs to him. I still kept quiet waiting for him to finish his well-rehearsed speech.

"So, Major, what do you have to say?"

I stood erectly at parade rest, looked into his eyes, and said, *"No, thank you, sir. I found a job elsewhere, and I will be leaving this post today."*

He looked at me with a stunned glare and retorted, *"In that case, Major, we have nothing further to discuss."*

I snapped to attention, saluted, did a sharp about-face and marched proudly out the door, making sure I shut it gently, and headed down the hallway out of the headquarters forever. I could see the awe on the faces of the other officers as I left the office. I was ecstatic as I walked briskly back to my room. The look on that general's face was a sight to behold. He was furious with me, and he made it quite obvious that higher powers had contacted him and jumped in his britches. He was one upset general. I laughed all the way to my room. I complimented myself on successfully keeping my mouth shut in the presence of the general and his court-masters. Another crazed white senior officer bites the dust after trying to create man-made trenches especially for me.

I stopped by the PMO and said my good-byes to the people I had met and wished them luck. They were sad to see me leave, but they understood my reasoning. This general would not give me a fair shake at doing my job, and his eyes told me he was a vindictive man. I would have made a good provost marshal at this post, but it obviously was not meant to be. I packed up my things and quickly departed Aberdeen, contacted the MP branch, and told them where I would be staying while awaiting their instructions for my report date to Fort Detrick.

Weeks later I discovered that the two-star general contacted a black male LTC stationed in Texas and asked him to be his PM. Seems this guy worked for the general once before, and the LTC accepted the job. "Now you tell me what was in that general's mind as it applied to me? It doesn't sound like it had to do with race. What was it then?" I will never know or understand where he was coming from.

On the ride to my new home, I thought about this unnecessary confrontation with the general and felt uneasiness churning within. I had won another battle, but winning did not cushion the thoughts that raced through my mind. Why did I, or anyone for that matter, have to continuously face man-made inequities in the military environment? I was constantly judged by someone before they even met me. My performance records told my military history, yet look how many people had ignored this and merely treated me outright like a person of no worth based on race, sex, age, and rank. When would it ever end?

During the past ten years, I had confrontations with ten military officers, who had tried to get me to bite the dust and accept their planned failure for my life. *Now was this sick or what?* I thought about the young black female captain that would have been my deputy at Aberdeen and wondered how in the world she would survive the hard road ahead. How many valleys would she be pushed into before she had to call it quits? She appeared to be a go-getter and a very conscientious soldier, but would she be able to protect herself from evil and the hidden injustices that were rampant in the male military environment? I was older and wiser on my second time around entering the military, yet look at all the trials and tribulations I had to endure for ten years. How was a naive, immature young soldier supposed to make it through those lions' dens that he/she was destined to run up against? How many have already bitten the dust based on someone's mad craze with the stroke of the pen on an evaluation report? It is pathetic and pitiful.

General Cadoria eventually called me and asked if I was really satisfied about taking the job at Fort Detrick. The MP branch had some other jobs available for me equivalent to my rank, but they were in Kansas and Missouri. I told her that the assignment at Fort Detrick would suffice, since all I planned to do now was to simply slide through the next few years I had left until retirement. I informed her that I'd had enough of these blatant inequities, and I was tired of fighting unnecessary battles. I thanked General Cadoria for her expedient assistance and extended my love and best wishes to her. She told me to continue to hang in there and, if I needed her, to just call. Not once did she try to convince me that I should change my thoughts about the military, based on the continuous inequities I met. Normally, she would preach to me about how good the military was. But not this time because it seems that she had a conflict with a navy admiral, who was her rater, and had given her a bad OER.

How can we have faith in the military system that says *be all that you can be in the army,* while some manic-depressive white male lurks in the shadows waiting to beat you to the ground? I'm sorry, but the military system did not treat women fairly and permitted too many inequities to exist during my tour in the army. Being a black female was hazardous, and there is no other way to put it. General Cadoria retired the same year as I did with her one star, not two stars, on her shoulders. She was downtrodden, tired, very ill—a wounded woman. But I truly think she feels the same as I do—she is more diplomatic and tactful than I. God is the only answer; and all rewards, praise, and redemption come only from him. The only way to make it through this complex world and an insane, unhealthy working environment is to maintain your faith in God and only him because the human element will fail you nearly every time.

I often fear missing the reason I was born, knowing God's perfect will for me, and the danger of making wrong choices that will make my life less than maximum. How can I be sure if I'm doing what God wants me to do? I always refer to Romans 12:1-2 when I get confused about my place and purpose in this confused, complex Promised Land. *"Do not conform to this world, but be transformed by the renewing of your mind, that you may prove what is good and acceptable and the perfect will of God."* I have nothing more to prove to myself or anyone during my remaining military journey.

As I wrote my book and inserted my OER ratings, I had completely forgotten all the things I had accomplished during my twenty-one years on active duty. As I remembered all the valleys I encountered during those years and shared them with you in this book, I still feel some anger. After my confrontation with the two-star general at Aberdeen, I thought about my two-star guardian angel, General Curry, in Frankfurt, Germany. *Why did God expose me to two completely opposite generals within such a short span of time?* Within weeks, I went from an experience with an angel overseas to one with a devil Stateside.

I went to a bookstore and bought the book written by General Curry's wife, entitled *The General's Lady,* which covers their life up to 1981. My daughter asked me to send her a copy of the book because she also liked the general through her contacts with him. As I read her book, I knew why this man (angel) had crossed my path. Mrs. Curry tells the story of their long climb to the Pentagon and shares the very special secret of power and authority. Throughout her book, she relates the strong religious influence General Curry's mother had on his life: *"I know my son, Jerry, has received the Lord Jesus and asked him to take charge of his life because I was there when it happened."* His mother told him to "look to Jesus to help you in the stressful situations that are bound to rise." The Currys knew that God had a plan for them and sensed that all they needed to do was to be faithful and trust in him. Even the hardships were part of the preparation.

Mrs. Curry noted that the general's favorite scripture was Isaiah 40:31: *"Those who wait upon the Lord will mount up with wings as eagles, that they shall run and not be weary, and they shall walk and not faint."* He explained to his children that in this life there are two kinds of people: sparrows and eagles. Sparrows flock together, trying to please their peers while an eagle has chosen to stand alone, above the common flock in order to follow the highest calling God has for him/her.

The *nice guys* seem to be too few in the army that I served, but I now know that God was with me always. Then I read on to discover that General Curry took command of none other than Aberdeen Proving Grounds a few years earlier—the same post that I arrived at in 1984 with the madman in charge. I couldn't believe it. I estimated it was in the late '70s or early '80s that General Curry was in command. It could have been that General Curry, who was God-sent to this earth, was followed in command by the two-star general from hell, who gave me such grief. What a coincidence. At least God let me cross paths with General Curry while assigned in Germany in 1983-84. The good guys and gals don't have a chance unless they put everything in God's hands and proceed through life with complete faith. There is no other way. I thank God that I met Major General Curry. He definitely had an impact on this homegirl.

In September 2006, I searched the Web and found an article that read "Mr. Curry retired after a thirty-four-year army career in which he rose from the rank of private to major general and became the new chief of the National Highway Traffic Safety Admin istration (NHTSA)." "A Black Man in a White Man's Arm X," as he titled an essay published in 1981, Mr. Curry found the path to promotion steep. "The rules favor the majority," he wrote. "But in the United States, this only means that minorities must work harder and pay a higher price."

Hallelujah . . . I never knew that General Curry had written this article until this year and am in awe that he more or less substantiates what I have written in my book about *a black woman in the white man's army*. I rest my case as I continue to wrap up my story. ***God is good***.

CHAPTER 12

My True Love: Music

Being the music lover that I am, I always seemed to find a way to play music and entertain wherever my travels took me. Just because I didn't make it as a big-time entertainer in the '70s did not mean that I had to give up my music completely. Why waste such talents? After I returned to active duty in 1974, I formed a dynamic four-piece all-female band with members from the WAC army band at Fort McClellan and named our group Free Spirit. Karen played guitar, Goldie on drums, Mona on sax, Blue on piano, and I played the bass and did the vocals. Ironically, I was the only one who could not read music, but they needed

a little soulful boost in ad-libbing; thus, I served that purpose. We practiced often, arranged enough songs to play three sets, and began performing on and off post. Everyone enjoyed our music, and we played army songs, rhythm and blues, country, rock, and polkas.

I was the only officer in the band and some jealous, cruel people tried to accuse me of fraternizing with enlisted women. These sick-minded people tried their best to destroy our group rather than give us support. But we were professional soldiers on the job, very talented musicians, and gained respect and encouragement from the majority of our friends and associates. An article about our band was written in the Fort McClellan newspaper, and some of the comments were *"Lieutenant Lindsey,*

73

commander of company B has formed a women's band who call themselves Free Spirit, and in the words of Lieutenant Lindsey, 'We don't use written music, so we play what we feel.' Lieutenant Lindsey has never given up her music. She said, 'Sometimes I just take my guitar outside and play. The trainees sit around, and we sing and have a good time.' She gathered up fellow music lovers on post and formed the group whose motto is 'Go with the flow and let the spirit run free.' As long as there are music lovers on post, Lieutenant Lindsey will have a band."

Our all-female combo continued performing for three years until I shipped out to my next assignment. In the future, I would team up with these female musicians at WAC reunions; and we would jam at Karen's house, recapturing the good old music days at McClellan. In 2005, I went to the fiftieth reunion at Fort Lee, Virginia. It had been ten years since I attended these reunions. Upon my arrival, I surprisingly learned that many of my WAC buddies thought that I was dead. Somehow, my demise had been mistaken for another WAC who unfortunately had passed due to breast cancer. Karen, the guitar player, immediately approached me smiling from ear to ear, gave me a big bear hug, and placed the bass guitar in my hands. The combo ended up entertaining the reunion attendees for three days with our soul jamming music.

I met two new dynamic musicians at this reunion who really added spice to the combo. Karen played sax, and this chick could blow her horn. Jan played keyboards, and her little fingers tickled those keys so soulfully. She looked at me while we were jamming and said, *"It sure is nice to play music with someone who has risen from the dead."* This combo simply seemed to gel; everyone indicated that they enjoyed our music, and a good time was had by all. We hope to provide the same combo music at the 2007 WAC reunion in Branson, Missouri. It is so neat to perform with talented female musicians.

During my assignment in Germany, I formed a four-piece jazz band and kept the name Free Spirit. The combo was comprised of myself on vocals and bass, Frank on piano, Mike on drums, and Pierre on sax. These guys could cook, and playing for European people was so refreshing because they were an attentive audience who truly appreciated jazz and rhythm and blues.

It was great to have talented German musicians sit in and play with our group. I loved playing in a small jazz club located in a cobblestone alley in the heart of downtown Frankfurt. Our band performed for military affairs on post, and we moved around off post playing in German nightclubs. We even did gigs on boat rides down the river Rhine. I became very popular in the music arena and even had an offer from a music agent from France. He wanted me to pack up my bags and go with him to his country to pursue a big-time music career. Believe me, it was very tempting, but I had a military career to complete (unfinished business).

I probably had a good chance of recognition in Europe as a vocalist and bassist; black female entertainers have a better chance abroad than they do in the States. I often think of how Tina Turner, who happens to be my age, made her start overseas. She eventually received her well-deserved recognition that she struggled so hard to attain in the States. *What would have happened if I had been brave enough to pursue my love of music in France? Would my biggest dream of playing music professionally have become a reality? Oh well, I'll never know.*

I cherish those music days at Fort McClellan and in Germany because they were the highlights of my love for entertaining. Whenever I played music, it was like flying on a cloud. I would feel so high after a gig, and it would take me hours to *come down* after a job. Once I returned to the States in 1984, my music-entertainment days seemed to dissipate. I couldn't find musicians who were willing to sacrifice the time and effort it takes in putting together a good band.  Those I met wanted to play music solely to make money without commitment and practice. I eventually had to give up my love for music and settle for jamming with others whenever it presented itself. Music is indeed my first love and something that I would truly enjoy doing the rest of my life, but I don't know what the future will bring in this area. **God, thank you, for blessing me with this talent.**

CHAPTER 13

All-Army Softball

My second love was playing softball, which I began at the age of eight. My mother was a great softball player and took me to all her games, and that's how I became such a good athlete. From middle school through high school, I was one dynamic female softball player. Being a female athlete was taboo during my era in comparison to what opened up for female athletes in the '80s. Then in the '90s, women could pursue professional sports in basketball, softball, soccer, etc. I often feel that I was born ahead of my time in the many endeavors I wanted to pursue. Such is life.

As a young twenty-one-year-old enlistee in the army in 1961, I could freely exhibit my softball talents. I was an outstanding shortstop and had no difficulty in outshining other teammates, and I received recognition and write-ups in the Fort McClellan and Fort Sam newspapers about my talents: *"Sergeant Byrd belts a ball and a tune (music) with equal virtuosity. And in both her full-time activities, she furnishes entertainment for many people. A platoon sergeant for WAC students in courses at the medical school, Sergeant Byrd plays softball with the WAC team on which she is a grandstand player and a spectators' favorite. She socks many balls out of the park and stops the hard-line drives that come at her shortstop position."*

Another article with me photographed with the post commanding general read *"The colorful Brooke Army Medical Center shortstop, Sergeant Byrd, copped the most valuable player award in the women's division. Byrd played outstanding defensive ball and was a whirlwind when it came to hitting. The score remained tied until the seventh inning when Byrd, who was already playing a beautiful defensive game at short, came to the plate. The outfielders moved back, as if she were Maris, and Byrd proceeded to bloop the ball over the second baseman's head and made the full tour of the bases, literally outrunning the ball for a grand-slam homer."*

Playing slow-pitch softball on the army teams was actually boring for me, so I tried out for a civilian fast-pitch team hosted by the owner of the Pepsi-Cola plant in San Antonio. Fast-pitch was more challenging, and I won the shortstop berth on this semiprofessional team. I've mentioned this in an earlier chapter but wish to recapture a memorable event during this period. One of our team's major highlights was participating in a tournament in Mexico City during the 1968 Olympics. We chartered a bus, toured the city, and played outstanding ball against our opponents. Despite the fact that I suffered from diarrhea from eating Mexican food and drinking the water, this was one of the most rewarding experiences for me at age twenty-three.

During my break in service, I continued to play fast-pitch softball on some great teams in DC. I truly enjoyed this sport, learned more softball techniques, traveled a lot, and had great fun with my second love. When I returned to active duty in 1974, I had to resort back to playing slow-pitch softball because the army never switched over to fast-pitch. I continued to excel at the sport while stationed at Fort McClellan, including being player-coach of the post team. We participated in tournaments all over the South and mideastern states at other military posts. We always returned home with the winning trophy, and I managed to get the Most Valuable Player Award quite often. Once again, articles in the post newspapers were written about my athletic attributes.

I truly loved playing softball, and it gave me a similar feeling I received when playing music; I simply loved to play and entertain, as if it were in my blood. In 1976, my superiors and teammates suggested that I try out for the all-army softball team hosted yearly at Fort Indiantown Gap, Pennsylvania. I was reluctant at first to try out for this prestigious team because of my age (thirty-five) and my reduced speed due to the knee injury I sustained a year before. But I gave in and went to this summer camp and found myself wrapped up in a maze of excitement and confusion. I was a captain and one of two officers trying out for the team. The other women who showed up at camp were so competitive. I could hardly believe my eyes; they were ruthless young vultures, who wanted to make the team at any expense. During camp tryouts, we spent the entire day for over a month in training (running, exercising, and softball practice) until dark. I ended up being housemother in our barracks to these killer women. The coach blessed me with this job based on my age and rank; however, he really did not do me a favor. I struggled to keep up physically and emotionally in an effort to make the team. The running

and constant physical requirements took its toll on my knees, legs, and ankles. Coupled with this physical pain, I had to emotionally tend to all the backstabbing and sheer chaos that occurred in the barracks at night. Some of the players tried to suck up to me, thinking I could help them make the team. Others even offered their bodies to the male coach in order to make it. I don't know if he gave in or not. I was too tired and worn-out to really care, one way or another.

When it came time to cut the twenty-five tryouts down to twelve, holy hell erupted. I never saw so many tears, yells, curses, and what have yous from so many grown women. The other officer that tried out for the team was my pitcher on the Fort McClellan team. She was cut from the team and she flipped. I tried to alert her from the beginning that it would be a lot of pressure, but she wouldn't listen to me. I knew before we arrived at camp that she would not have the stamina to make the team, but I did not want to discourage her. She mistakenly thought that because we won so many games as a McClellan team, she was a good pitcher. She was not physically fit, slightly overweight, and a mediocre player. It was the players behind her that made things click. She cried profusely when she was cut from the team and gave me all her softball equipment and told me that she was giving up softball completely. She returned to McClellan downtrodden and ego devastated. I felt very sorry for her.

I managed to make the team, but not as a shortstop. The constant pounding on my knees and legs slowed me down immensely, so I tried out for first base and made the team. I actually enjoyed playing this position that I never played before. The coach needed me not only as his assistant coach but also because I had a big bat. He was the one who suggested I try out for first base. The final twelve women on the team proved to be awesome, and we played some good softball. This experience proved to be another challenge in my life that I will never forget. When I returned to McClellan, a newspaper article covered the results of my experience on the all-army team. *"In 1976, the women's sports program at McClellan probably involved more women and produced more championship female athletes than any other army post. When an individual from Fort McClellan is selected for an all-army team, it's big news; but Captain Lindsey made even bigger news when she was named an all-American at the national softball tournament this year. Lindsey was a*  *star player on the Women's Intramural League and later played as a member of the all-army team that participated in the National Class A Softball Championship in York, Pennsylvania. The army team finished as the tournament's runner-up against a field of forty-seven teams from around the nation, and Lindsey, the army's big gun, was tabbed as an all-American as a result of her performance.*

The army team, competing in its first ever national tournament, won seven of nine games and was the only squad to defeat the champion Rustic Bar, Minnesota, team. Apparently, Lindsey did something right at York, Pennsylvania. The honors she received there confirmed the belief of many people here that she ranks among the finest softball players in the army. After all, Lindsey now has

the trophies to prove that she is one of the best softball players in the nation. That's not bad news for someone from way out at Fort McClellan, Alabama, either."—Fort McClellan News

Being in partnership with God, I know that anything is possible.

Once I was assigned overseas, my softball pursuits flourished. I continued to excel in softball as a first baseman and assisted in bringing home trophies on the Frankfurt post team. We were the champion European female softball team in the three years I played on the team. Our team traveled all over Europe, whipped on all the other army teams. My trophy collection grew as I continued to participate in one of my greatest loves at the very young age of forty-three.

When I returned Stateside, softball enjoyment began to dwindle. I could not find competitive teams to play on and ended up playing shortstop on C or D teams, which was very boring for me. I continued to play on mediocre teams in Maryland, Georgia, and Alabama, but the thrill was gone; the excitement; good, fast softball playing; and the spirit of the game diminished. I gave up the sport at age fifty-three; that is, until I find a competitive team to play with.

My love for music and softball filled any void I had in my relationships and military career. All I ever really wanted to do was to entertain as a musician and be an athlete. I truly believe that was my calling, but somehow I never reached the heights I felt I should have attained. But I must thank God for blessing me with these talents and giving me the opportunity to enjoy the pleasures that music and softball brought into my life. I count my blessings daily.

CHAPTER 14

It Ain't Over till It's Over!

I had accepted a job at Fort Detrick, Maryland, that was not commensurate to my rank, but I couldn't stay at Aberdeen and work for a madman. I would not be selected for schooling that would assist me in getting promoted, and I only had five more years to go, three of which would be spent at Fort Detrick, leaving me only one more assignment to overcome. I did the best that I could do up to this point, and I had to accept this fact. My business was almost complete. *What is ahead of me now?*

Well, my new job was indeed a challenge. I became the provost marshal on a 1,216-acre installation with over three thousand personnel, 73 percent of which were civilian. Most tenant organizations were engaged in research and development, which used highly sensitive and/or infectious material, with a quad-service medical-logistics management and communication center. This center was a key army facility, which carried presidential, department of state, and department of defense (DOD) traffic. It also provided technical assistance for the contract-operated United States-USSR *hotline* on the post.

I walked into my new job to find myself surrounded by thirty to forty DOD-

civilian police and two MP-enlisted men. These policemen were considered by others on post as *security officers* in blue uniforms with guns on hips, having no expertise in police matters. They were not respected; most of them were out of shape, uneducated, downright lazy, and white. I immediately faced friction because most of the DOD policemen had been there for ages and had snowballed and walked all over the young female captain who had just departed. They were not ready for a mature, no nonsense older black chick like me. I indeed had my work cut out for me, and I had 100 percent support from my new commander, Colonel Hoke, a medical-corps officer, who insisted that I charge ahead and make whatever changes I deemed necessary. My immediate supervisor was also a medical-corps black colonel, and he was a very nice man, who also gave me his full support. My MP bosses were located at Fort Sam Houston, Texas. So I was back to working for *nice* guys. There is a God!

My first task was to get rid of my right-hand man, the civilian chief of police, who insisted on giving me havoc instead of helping me. He had been there for ten years or more, was a downright Maryland redneck, and tried his best to create a valley to push me in. He was supported by a few good ole boys who were from the same redneck area as he was. I was a master of battle by now, after my confrontation with a two-star general; and for once I was the boss of all police matters. These guys really didn't have a chance against me.

My OER for the first year at Fort Detrick tells the story. My immediate boss stated: *"Major Lindsey brought to the PM office extraordinary expertise and experience. She is well versed in the didactic phases of crime prevention and law enforcement. She was successful in upgrading federal-policeman positions and police equipment—a feat, which appeared impossible before her arrival. Supervisory levels of the PMO made quantum improvement by her exact tasking and subsequent removal of key personnel who stifled personnel management. Organization of the PMO was accomplished, establishing a training officer position which resulted in upgrading training requirements.*

Police job requirements were rewritten and performance standards defined so that evaluations are quantifiable and articulated in a substantive manner; physical-security program improved, and criminal-investigation activities increased despite austere resources. Particularly noteworthy was coordination of an antithreat test at post in conjunction with the local FBI field office. Morale and motivation to be a top cop *were enhanced. Major Lindsey should be selected for attendance at the Armed Forces Staff College and subsequently assigned to ever-increasing responsibility at MACOM or DA level. I strongly urge promotion to LTC at the earliest."*

Colonel Hoke wrote*: "Major Lindsey possesses a great deal of prior experience and it shows. The professionalism of the federal police force has vastly improved due to her setting performance standards and then enforcing them. The* deadwood *leadership has been cleaned out and vacancies backfilled with competent personnel who know their business. As a result, we are receiving applications for personnel who want to be policemen, as opposed to taking a job to get a foot in the workforce door. Cooperation with the FBI and other federal, state, county, and city-law enforcement agencies is at an all-time high. She is LTC material now, so make her one soonest. Just leave her here after you do that."*

Oh, how good it felt to be back to normal, doing what I do best . . . meeting a challenge head-on and making the best out of a mess. My bosses were great, and I was having a good time performing my job. I got through my next year with another outstanding OER. I had a new immediate boss, a black colonel, who was all right; but he was not as professional as the colonel who departed for a Fort Sam assignment. He stated: *"Major Lindsey managed and motivated an understrength DOD police element with confidence, discerning judgment and exceptional professional competence. She is extremely innovative and proactive and initiated training programs which enhanced proficiency of policemen and concurrently improved the readiness posture of reserve component IRR personnel undergoing annual training at Fort Detrick. Her other accomplishments included actively seeking means to augment the DOD police force, instituting PMO automation as it relates to offense reporting, vehicle registration, crime statistics, National Crime Information Center, and administration through use of state-of-the-art equipment. She effectively assessed employee resources, strengths, and competencies; hired a new police chief; and selected new shift supervisors who, under her guidance, have assisted subordinates in the elevation of skills, knowledge, attitudes."*

And Colonel Hoke further stated: *"Major Lindsey weathered a storm of bad luck extremely well. She had taken the proper action to weed out the* dead wood *in her civilian police force. However, before she could even recruit for vacancies, I got hit with a personnel cut and a formal end-strength constraint. Consequently, she had to live with what she had for eight months, which included a vacant chief of police position. To offset this, she arranged for on-call support from the Frederick City Police, which gave some assurance to patrols that they would have backup. Promote to LTC. Just don't take her away when you do."*

My MP colonel boss at Fort Sam retired in 1986 and wrote a nice letter for my file stating *"This letter is to thank you for making my job easy as well as productive. In the MP Corps, we quickly learn that the absence of crisis is an important measure of how well we are performing. We become accustomed to* crisis management *and often forget that our mission is much broader. Certainly, we have had problems, but they were short-lived and of minimal magnitude; and I credit this to your leadership, ingenuity, and your willingness to give that extra 10 percent that spells the difference between mere survival and true accomplishment. As the installation provost marshal, you have become intently aware of the post's unique sensitivities and vulnerabilities. Your initiatives have already caused considerable improvement, and I have every confidence that the momentum you have attained will continue until vulnerability has been minimized. Just as noteworthy has been the personnel improvements you have made. Against all odds, you have succeeded in terminating some adversarial police officers and have made much progress toward building a police force with professionalism, enthusiasm, and genuine concern for police community relations. Your achievements have been commendable, and you have every right to be proud. Thank you and please accept my best wishes for continued success."*

Man, I had busted butt the past two years on a post with little crime problems, but with ongoing drug dealings. The main problem was physical security of all buildings based on the terrorist threats statewide at the time. I automated every activity in the PMO, and the operations section looked like the deck of Star Trek with my desk sergeant appearing to be Captain Kirk in charge of all controls. I acquired the newest automated police equipment available for my guys and upgraded physical security measures. "I was on an upward roll until—guess what? Yeah, the good guys received orders to ship out—both of my bosses had new assignments. Out walked the nice, angelic guys and in walked—you got it—two demons from hell. When would this cycle ever end?"

Initially, my new medical-corps bosses seemed to be all right as they concentrated more on getting settled into their turfs and new jobs. So I was left alone for a while to continue upgrading physical security standards on post. I went to Fort Gordon for my Christmas leave; and when I returned after New Year in 1988, the shit had hit the fan.

During my absence, three malcontent police officers tried to discredit my staff personnel and me. It seems that some of my people were accused of falsifying Christmas-leave time cards; I was accused of knowing such and supporting them. The new guys at command level agitated the situation by escalating the incident from an IG complaint to an AR 15-6 investigation, to a full-blown CID investigation conducted by an idiot. My staff and I were fingerprinted and treated like hardened criminals. Man, how your own kind, MPs, can turn on you in a heartbeat. The entire investigation was ludicrous, and there was nothing I could do to stop it. My new MP boss at Fort Sam couldn't or wouldn't do anything, so I had to grit my teeth and bear it all for six long months.

My staff and I went through pure hell; we could do no good as malcontents continued to try to stab us in the back, and in the end my credibility as a leader had been marred. Rumors spread over Fort Peyton Place. My staff and I became defensive; we watched our backs, constantly thinking everyone was out to get us; and eventually bitterness and negativism became rampant with us.

The investigation ended after six months with the final report showing no criminal offense. *We were proved innocent—yippee. But did it stop there—hell no!* The new guys from hell still felt we were guilty of a wrongdoing, wanted to appease CID for the long hours they put into the investigation, and decided to punish us anyway. The post commander gave us all letters of administrative reprimands to appease their personal minds; and after that action, they felt that the case was then closed—subjects guilty and sentenced accordingly. "Swatting a fly with a hammer."

My staff and I refused to take all this lying down and rebutted using various outlets (USACARA, DAIG, and the senator of Maryland). I compiled the longest rebuttal I'm sure the DAIG ever received in their lifetime. Ironically, one of my homeboys from the MPOA course, a black major, was the action officer and said he would keep me updated on my complaint. My chief of police also submitted a DAIG complaint in conjunction with mine. This DAIG-report investigation continued on into my next assignment after I departed Fort Detrick.

During these mind-boggling months, I became so bitter and negative with my work, at the command level, and just about all others around me on the installation. It was like déjà vu back in Frankfurt before I departed V Corps. I had worked so hard for two long years making improvements, being praised with two outstanding OERs and a letter, and going over and beyond the call of duty. All of this hard work, only to face another injustice created by a few police officers. I had refused to give positions of higher authority to these men, based on their lack of expertise, and had to deal with two medical-corps commanders, who really didn't know what the hell they were doing. Nevertheless, I guess they felt like flapping their powerful wings as colonels and tried so hard to make a mountain out of a molehill. They actually felt they were doing the right thing and wanted me to be their scapegoat. It was as if this was the most excitement they had ever had in their medical field.

By this time, I knew that I was so far gone on the negative deep end, and that if I did not regroup quickly, I was destined to perish. I prayed, meditated, wrote lengthy spiritual inspirations in my journal, and felt that I had to do something to help myself. I begged the MP branch to get me off the post before I really did something stupid. I was one hot firecracker ready to explode. I did not deem this request to ship out as a matter of running away, but as a matter of survival because I was not strong enough to fight anymore. This episode didn't make any sense because I was innocent of all charges with a supportive investigation and still being wrongfully accused and punished. I was fed up and ready to quit. I was tired of fighting these unnecessary battles in my assignments. *I was sick and tired of being sick and tired.*

CHAPTER 15

My Journey Begins to Wind Down

My military journey was coming to a definitive closing. Once I mentally made a choice to retire, I began feverishly planning for it by sending out resumes, checking job announcements, etc. I was revitalized in my efforts, despite many frustrating discoveries of the difficulties that faced me in finding a civilian job that I would enjoy. But since I was approaching this new goal with a positive attitude, any disappointment could be a closed door that would open up for challenges. I was getting back to my vibrant old self again and continuously prayed to God for guidance, strength, and job direction. I began to approach work with a sense of humor, practiced patience, and avoided responding to trivial matters defensively. I had to keep telling myself, "With faith in God, everything will be all right!" I had to have a daily positive visualization and move forward with an *all is well* feeling permeating every part of my being.

In August 1988, a disappointment slapped me in the face when I discovered that I had miscalculated my retirement date. I thought I would be getting out earlier, but my effective date wasn't until October 1989; I was eight months off target. My first response was that of frustration, but I regrouped and realized it was not catastrophic. This simply meant that I would be reassigned to another post and had a year to work on goal setting before my retirement. The important issue was that I would be changing jobs and my environment, and for once in my life, I could concentrate on my own needs. My branch decided to assign me to Fort Gordon, Georgia, and at the time it did not matter what the job would be because I only had eight more months to do until retirement.

A buddy of mine from DC called and asked me to go with her to play softball with a civilian team scheduled to participate in the Softball Nationals in Lexington, South Carolina. Before jumping the gun, I talked and prayed to God about it. I thought it would not be wise because I might injure myself. However, I decided to participate in the softball tournament, thinking that a change of environment from Fort Detrick and doing something I enjoyed would be good medicine for me. I took my books and journal with me, so I could continue my meditation.

The members of the team were very nice young ladies and had high aspirations of winning the softball tournament. I rode to South Carolina with my old softball friend from the Frankfurt days. BB and I had never played with this team, and our guess was that we were probably the best players on the team, based on age and experience. Once we arrived at the hotel, we met everyone and settled in for the night. I woke up early at 5 AM, dressed, and found a nice, quiet place in the hotel lounge and began reading and praying to receive God's message as to his will for me this Labor Day weekend.

To my surprise a message came to me during my reading: "I need a spiritual mind-set instead of an earth mind-set aided by the Holy Spirit. I must constantly act and live in ways that keep my mind at peace in Christ. Let the peace of Christ rule in your hearts."—Colossians 3:15 The reading went on to say that a rule means an *umpire* to arbitrate or to decide. This caught my attention since I was at a softball tournament. I kept reading: "Christ's peace in my life should be the umpire, deciding authority. I must clothe myself with compassion, kindness, humility, gentleness, and patience." The message urged me to let Christ's peace be my umpire and be very watchful of what deepens that peace or begins to rob it. That blessed peace would guide me sweetly but firmly in what to do and not to do, what to say or not to say. God delivered this message at the right time.

I enjoyed that holiday weekend, despite the fact our team was eliminated from the tournament after two games. I was anxious to return to Maryland to concentrate on my new assignment. I decided to pamper and treat myself by purchasing a big screen TV and an XT Turbo computer and printer before I left Fort Detrick. A gay friend of mine was in the computer business and made me a very good offer. I always wanted my own computer because I had become very proficient with it after my experience in complete automation of the PMO. Through self-teaching and exploration, I had learned some automated operations that would pay off for me in the future. This purchase proved to be one of the best investments I ever made in my life and became the beginning of my interest in learning everything I could about this new technology.

Chantay and Damiano got married in Copenhagen in 1984 and decided they wanted to return to the United States in 1986. I was happy to have them stay with me in Germantown during my Fort Detrick assignment. Damiano found a job as a welder, and Chantay attended a word-processing school in Maryland. We were one happy family again and made trips to visit my mother often. After I returned from my softball trip on Labor Day, I had a long discussion with Chantay and Damiano. Something within told me to give them the option of going to Georgia with me to live. Their marriage was getting rocky, and I thought that maybe changing environments would help; and they would find a way to make things work. I told them to think about it; Chantay

had a long talk with her granny, and within a day or so, they decided to uproot and move to Georgia with me. Life was a risk and a challenge for them also.

I kept up with my readings and prayed for guidance from God. I did not want to make wrong decisions in my life. There would be times when I would not make the right decision and misinterpret what God really wanted me to do. However, I was functioning much better with this new mind-set.

During mid-September, I was involved in going-away luncheons at Fort Detrick. Everyone wanted to say good-bye in their own way and present me with gifts. I felt blessed to have true friends come forth and wish me good luck and happiness after my traumatic experience at this installation. It made me feel so good to see how many people truly loved and respected me outside of my immediate work environment. My luncheon given by command (my very nice bosses who tried to slam-dunk me) was scheduled during this time. Since everyone else was giving me a going-away party, command scheduled this so they could *save face*. I was required to attend, although I requested that they not give me a going-away luncheon.

I discovered that a very dear friend of mine was assigned at Fort Richie as a commander. Dorothy Spencer was raised near my hometown and had attained the rank of colonel, and she knew me during my early entertaining days when I played music with her uncle in Monessen and Donora. *It's a small army, isn't it?* I tracked her down and asked her to please try to attend my going-away luncheon scheduled by command. We talked over old times, and I gave her a short synopsis of what had transpired with me the past year. Well, Dorothy, bless her heart, showed up and made my day. I put on my smiley, devious face for the command and purposely failed to tell them about my colonel friend, who showed up unannounced.

I scurried around introducing Dorothy to my friends and the two backstabbing bosses, and they were astounded. Obviously, it had been a long time since either one of them had seen a black female colonel, other than a nurse. Dorothy was invited to join us at the head table, her on one side of me and my slayer on the other. I was subjected to speeches by my police officers, softball players, and friends—most of them roasting me in fun. My two-faced boss made the mistake of asking Dorothy to say something, since she was a friend from way back. *Why did he do that?* Colonel Spencer was the orator of all orators, and she literally took the show away from command. My mean ole bosses were upstaged by a five-foot-three black female colonel, who told it like it was.

I had one of my police officers videotape the entire luncheon, and it is a film to behold—downright precious. Dorothy had me in tears as she blurted out her dynamic speech in my honor. God had surely sent her to ease the subdued hurt and pain within my soul! She astounded the guests with a testimonial speech of all speeches that washed away all the inequities I had experienced during my entire military career. I was no longer hostile or angry, and I let it all flow away as I listened to Dorothy speak. I thanked God for sending this genuine, blessed friend to ease my soul. My last days at Fort Detrick were ending on a positive, spiritual note. After the luncheon, I thought all was well until I had another confrontation with my two bosses.

These guys were like Amos and Andrew—a white colonel and a black LTC. The LTC was initially a friend who supported me before the CID incident and suddenly turned on me and went along with whatever the colonel said and did. He had experienced racial injustice during his career but was now dishing his dirt by the bucketful on top of my head. How sad, indeed. Anyway, these guys wanted to disapprove the time I had allotted to out process, and they were not willing to give me the permissive time necessary to go to Augusta to find a house. I was so angry I could have burst. They insisted on giving me havoc up to the day I departed their command. Well, I backed off, tried to maintain my cool, let peace dwell within, and asked them what amount of time they were willing to approve so I could go house hunting.

We finally agreed that I could take five days TDY to take my car to Georgia, find a house (that I had already found a week ago), return to Fort Detrick, and have five more days to out process. My intuition told me a week ago to *do my thing* and find a place to live. All I had to accomplish now was to get my car to Augusta, arrange to have my utilities turned on, and find out what my new job would be. Despite this outlandish treatment by my military foes, I calmly agreed to the days allotted and left the post the next day for Georgia. I could make things work given the time span, and I would not let these idiots get the best of me now. I made good travel time on my way to Augusta and stopped in South Carolina for gas and bought a baseball cap that caught my attention which said *"God never fails . . . I'm proud to be a Christian!"* Amen. Spiritual signs kept popping up everywhere I went on my trip down South.

After arriving at a military friend's house whom I had previously contacted and coordinated my move with, I made arrangements for utility hookups in my house. Then I went to the personnel office on post to find out what my job assignment would be. I was told that I would be working with the International Military Training Division as a training officer responsible for training over three hundred international students annually from sixty nations. This sounded good to me, so I went to meet my new boss who was a civilian, GS-11, and quickly discovered that there was no doubt that we had opposite personalities, destined to clash. *Valley time on the horizon once again!*

Mr. Lynch (will refrain from using his real name) was a retired LTC, who had been in this job five or more years, was an obvious southern racist, and thought that he was a god. I immediately knew that I would be working for another madman. However, in a very peaceful voice and manner, I expressed my concern to him on being treated like a human being regardless of race, color, sex, age, or creed. I gave Mr. Lynch a very short synopsis of what I had been through the past ten years of my military career and indicated to him that I was not in the mood for any more bullshit from anyone.

I politely told him, *"I'm here to do a job, so just let me do it until I retire a year from now. You stay out of my hair, and I'll stay out of yours."*

As he spoke, it was not difficult to see what he was all about: a racist redneck, hot tempered with a philosophy of *no place for women in military*, reluctant to change, unhappy old man. Mr. Lynch expressed to me that he felt a woman should not have the job I was assigned to because his foreign students, mostly male officers, would probably rebel against me. His rationale was that most of the students were from countries where women cover their faces with veils and walk two steps behind their men. He was against me being the training officer but didn't have any choice in the matter. In a very calm mode, I stressed that I would worry about the job and these students after I got settled in my new home with my family. I didn't have to take this job because a GS-11 is equivalent to the rank of a major, and I was supposed to have a boss that outranked me by one rank or more. Despite the fact that I saw I would be dealing with another madman in my life, this didn't matter to me one bit. I was ready to relocate when informed of what the job was all about, viewed it as a challenging position, and opted to stick it out, while concentrating on my main priority, retire in one year to date. So be it! There was no need or desire on my part to battle, scream, shout, curse, or go into a defensive tactical mode. The man told me where he was coming from; he knew what I was all about, so let's simply get it on and over with. "Now is that a change in attitude or what? Of course, in the back of my active little mind, there was a voice saying so very empathetically: 'I will prove this man wrong about his perception of this job and of women, especially this black chick!' I had not flushed away the intriguing, cunning part of my being . . . that was still intact. Some things one cannot change."

I stopped in the Fort Gordon PMO to introduce myself to the guys in charge and met the PM, a white LTC and his deputy, a black major, who were very cordial. I shared my MP story with them, and the PM shockingly revealed his present dilemma. He was being forced to retire due to a CID investigation that was instigated by his own police officers internally. He was charged of showing favoritism to a high-ranking officer who assaulted someone in the officers' club. His people reported him; CID ran with it, trumped up charges against him, and now an LTC with twenty-six years of service was being forced to leave the system. I was astounded. I thought I was the only one being *dumped on* by the MP branch. The LTC was not receiving any support from command or the MP branch, so he was preparing for his retirement and was trying to maintain a positive attitude. He was planning to pack up, return to his home state, and become a civilian police officer. The MP branch seems to eat their folks alive.

I flew back to Maryland to arrange for my household shipment and to prepare for the return trip to Fort Gordon in five days. After the movers packed everything up, the kids and I proceeded on a caravan in our cars to Georgia. New opportunities were approaching my little family and me. My journey was coming to an end. *Would I manage to survive without an unnecessary struggle?*

CHAPTER 16

Unfinished Business, Finished!

Chantay, Damiano, and I got settled into our new home in Augusta. I went to work within a week, and Damiano found a job within two weeks; but Chantay was not having much luck in her job search. I told her to be calm and patient and that things will work out. Chantay could get depressed with a defeatist attitude at the drop of the hat.

As the training officer of international students, I found this job to be different from my MP duties, but interesting. We had a videotape recorder in our unit, so I got into videotaping all activities held for the students, which would later prove to be a worthwhile tool in my job. I was immediately sent on TDY to Dayton, Ohio, Wright Patterson Air Force Base for an orientation to my new job and met some new and interesting people. I ended up being Ms. Socialite and *favorite class member,* and they gave me a humorous certificate after the training was over. I even sat in with the band at the officers' club, played the bass, and sang some funky blues, while my classmates cheered me on. I had a good time on TDY and was even offered a higher position in the division by the civilian in charge of the overall international training program (one of Lynch's bosses). I told him I preferred to stay where I was and concentrate on my retirement.

Upon my return to Fort Gordon, I was approached by CID, who was still pursuing the Fort Detrick incident. They just wouldn't drop the case; and as a result of all this, my investigation was still on active file, even though charges were dropped. This meant that I had derogatory information actively floating around in my personnel file. I refused to be interrogated by CID, shook my head in dismay, and put it in the Lord's hands. I had not received word on the status of my DAIG complaint from my friend in DC. He contacted me months later, indicating that there was nothing they could do, so I just forgot it, since I would be retiring soon. By November, we were all settled into our new home, and the kids and I celebrated Thanksgiving by having a family dinner. We called my mother and discovered that she wanted to visit us for Christmas, so I sent her money for a bus ticket to Augusta and looked forward to having the entire family together again.

In December of 1988, I received a derogatory three-month OER from Fort Detrick by mail, requesting that I acknowledge receipt and sign it. I refused to sign a DA Form 67-8-1 before I departed Fort Detrick, which was an officer's evaluation form prep sheet that indicated my duties and responsibilities and how I felt I had performed my job. Nothing had changed on this form when I completed it for my annual rating. They could not give me an annual OER because I left before the year was over. All they could do was to give me a change of duty station OER, covering a three-month period. They did not have this OER completed before I departed; I had no idea what they were going to write, so I refused to sign another DA Form 67-8-1. **Note:** I had my named changed back to my maiden name in May 1988.

I became furious as I read the OER. The black LTC wrote: *"A talented officer whose ability is unlimited. Assigned missions or tasks were completed to perfection when they were consistent with her views. She does not accept command guidance in a constructive manner. She was extremely resourceful in improving the physical security of the installation. Her implementation of automation throughout the PMO improved accuracy and efficiency of traffic and crime management. Major Byrd refused to complete DA Form 67-8-1."*

I had to chuckle to myself as I continued to read his comments on my virtues: *"Quickly grasps concepts; does not seek to motivate and challenge subordinates equally; management style inhibits candor and frankness in subordinates; objects to command guidance and has the morality to speak out."*

Now does this sound paradoxical or what? My anger dissipated as I remembered how incompetent and two-faced this LTC was. I felt sorry for him because he was fighting for his career, and his ego needed him to get promoted, regardless of whom he trampled on in the process. Then I read the wishy-washy white colonel's remarks and really cracked up: *"Major Byrd is a fully capable and enthusiastic officer who does not fully accept command guidance. Very often her decisions and actions are driven by emotions rather than mission-oriented logic. She is extremely talented in automating functions that enhance efficiency and productivity. As for her potential, I would recommend assignments only in staff positions. She refused to complete DA Form 67-8-1."*

Now dig this. This is what the wishy-washy white colonel wrote on my annual OER as my senior rater before the CID investigation. *"Alert, articulate, and with a flair for innovation, Major Byrd has performed her PM duties in an outstanding manner. She is a team player whose selfless attitude has won her respect from subordinates and superiors alike. I especially prize her loyalty to her subordinates. With potential unlimited, I would heartily recommend her for those positions with increased responsibility at the MACOM or HQDA level."*

I won't even dwell upon the contradictions. "Now how could I change that fast and that drastically in my virtues and the performance of my duties within three months?" All I could do was pity these guys. They were still trying to stab me in the back and push me into a ditch. I called a military friend, told her about the OER, and she suggested that I write an appeal. I took her advice and wrote the following appeal to be included in my personnel record: *"I acknowledge receipt of your derogatory rating with the following comments: Subject report is obviously vindictive on the part of the rater and senior rater based on my formal DAIG complaint submitted against them in May. My DA Form 67-8-1 is dated 13 Jun 88, and nothing changed within three months. My OER was due 12 Jun 88, and I received the final rating on 14 Dec 88. My OER is not dated by my rater or senior rater, and it is ironic how my rating changed within three months. I submit that the derogatory OER is in retaliation based on my DAIG complaint, my secretary's congressional complaint, my criminal investigator's USACARA complaint, my chief of police's DAIG complaint, and my candor to stand up for my staff personnel, and my own rights and entitlements to justice."*

I never received any type of response on my appeal, so as far as I was concerned, the case was closed concerning everything revolving around the Fort Detrick incident. It didn't matter to me anymore. My career was coming to an end, and it was finally substantiated when I was called in to see my senior rater at Fort Gordon. He was an LTC (Lynch's immediate boss), and he informed me that I did not make the LTC promotion list. I didn't expect to be picked up, accepted it graciously, and would prepare to put in my retirement papers. He was very compassionate and tried to apologize for the way the military system had treated me because he had witnessed my professionalism and abilities as his training officer up to this point. I thanked him for his concern but told him all was well with me. ***When one door closes, a new one opens up!***

In December, I celebrated my forty-eighth birthday, and Chantay and Damiano took me out for a steak dinner. We also had cake and champagne at the house. I videotaped this event; I was a happy camper. Mom arrived in Augusta the day after my birthday, and we all had a blessed Christmas together. Mom and I went to visit a friend at Fort McClellan for a few days at Christmastime; she really enjoyed herself and met most of my retired WAC friends. We had a great time.

Chantay suggested that we take family portraits at the Augusta mall as a momentum of our holiday together. This was a great idea on her part, and I even videotaped our getting pictures taken. That precious family photo proudly hangs on my living room wall to this day. We all had a blessed and great time together. Mom truly enjoyed her visit and returned home for the New Year.

In February 1989, Damiano and I got Chantay a surprise cake for her twenty-third birthday, had champagne, and the three of us celebrated together. During this month, I started having serious gum problems and received extensive periodontal work. My neck began to cause me serious concern (injury from softball years before), so I finally went to the doctors. X-rays showed that my third and fourth vertebrae were deteriorating, and I had osteoporosis and arthritis in my neck. I immediately began therapy at the hospital with traction, stretching, and hot packs. I finally had a disk replacement in my neck in 2003 and have had no serious problems since.

I made several visits to Atlanta to check out the area as a possible place to retire and made some new friends. I attended a gay church, the Religious Science Church; met new folks; and bought some inspirational books and decided that Atlanta would be my choice to live upon retirement. I made contact with a friend who knew someone who could help Chantay in her job search. Chantay finally got a job as an assistant analyst on post with GTE/MSE, a telecommunications civilian-contract agency. She worked for a very nice retired CPT as his right hand gal and operated all administration and computer functions. This job would be the beginning for Chantay; she would do military contract work for years to come.

One of my main responsibilities as training officer was to persuade American Signal Corps students to sponsor each of my international students while taking the same course as they were. I had to convince these students to willingly take my guys and gals under their wings, help them in class, and show them the American way in social life. I used my video recorder to sell my pitch, have gobs of tapes to this day,  and it worked. I had no problems getting a sponsor for my students. My students were too much to handle at times, and they got into all kinds of trouble: driving while drinking, shoplifting, married students chasing after American women, complaints from sponsors about personal hygiene, failing classes, wife and children problems, or threat of war in their countries affecting them Stateside, on and on and on. Nevertheless, I tried to be there for each and they all knew that I was sincere in my efforts.

I stayed out of Mr. Lynch's way and avoided any conflict with him, so his cliché about my inability to interact positively with the students did not become a prophecy. The majority of the Middle Eastern students loved me to death and respected me as a woman; they walked two steps behind me. I was invited to visit Saudi Arabia, Kuwait, Egypt, Jordan, Turkey, anytime I deemed fit, knowing I would be welcomed by these students. I was showered with pictures and gifts and even got offers of marriage from several of my students; some of these guys were very rich.

However, the male students from Africa tended to shun me, and my aggressive manner was too much for them to endure based on their culture, I guess. But all in all, this was the perfect way to end my career, helping others and, in turn, learning so much about other cultures and countries. This was a very good shot in the arm for me, after all the valleys, ditches, and foxholes I had endured over the years.

The fun part of my new job consisted of exposing students to the American way of life, which included trips to Atlanta and Disney World in Orlando. I enjoyed these trips; the international students loved me, I loved them; and I videotaped everywhere we went. The students were great, and even Chantay enjoyed them; most of the younger foreign guys had a crush on her. The students gave us gifts from Israel, Philippines, Taiwan, Turkey, Jordan, Egypt, Spain, Venezuela, Saudi Arabia, Kuwait,  Belize, Kenya, and Tunisia. I worked hard on not getting into conflicts with Mr. Lynch and his screaming negative self—he got his kicks by shouting at people. With God's help, I endured the temptation to strike back in defense of the staff and my students.

One day out of the blue, Chantay decided to call her father in Charlotte, North Carolina. She wanted to see him after twenty long years and decided to visit him in June. She returned home very disappointed with her father. He lived with a woman with a houseful of kids, worked at the airport, and had a DWI so she had to drive him everywhere. He tried to impress Chantay, but she saw right through him. Obviously, he had not changed one bit. At least she decided for herself about her father, and I was glad she finally made that step.

Chantay and Damiano were constantly arguing, and their marriage was not getting any better. Chantay decided to put an end to it, got a lawyer, and paid $150 for a divorce. Damiano was devastated but knew that the marriage had failed. He moved into a trailer and continued working at the pizza place in Augusta. He finally became a naturalized citizen; bought his first pizza parlor a few years later; and, as of this date, is the proud father of a son and the owner of three pizza shops in Augusta, Georgia. To this day, he and Chantay keep in touch as friends, and he calls my mother at least once a year to see how she is doing. I am so very proud of Damiano and still refer to him as my son-in-law.

During this time frame, Chantay went to Colorado Springs to complete a contract job; and she was really excited—she drove to Colorado on her own. I cooked her some chicken, packed her a food bag, and helped her load the car. My daughter was venturing out on her own, facing life in an adventurous and challenging manner. She was becoming independent, self-sufficient, and self-reliant again. This was simply the beginning of her adventurous life in contract work; her travels during the past twenty years have taken her to so many places Stateside and overseas. As of this date, she is a GS-13 working at the Pentagon as a program systems analyst; but by the time this book is published, my dear daughter may be someplace else as she pursues upward mobility in the contracting world. Chantay has spent the majority of her career enduring constant obstacles in her path and dealing with men who believe that she does not belong in this field. You think I am a fighter; well, you should see my daughter do battle.

I started calling a few contacts in Atlanta, trying to find a job, but wasn't having much luck. I had four months to go before retiring, and I was starting to panic. I prayed nightly for God to show me the way. I read my *Daily Word*: "Feeling anxious about my future causes me to feel helpless now. I can determine my future experiences by evaluating and adjusting my present patterns of thinking, feeling, and acting. God's love supports me in every phase of living . . . and in a new beginning. Ask and I shall receive."

I had faith that all would be well. I visited friends in Atlanta, passed my resumes around, and made an appointment with Quest Associates, an outplacement agency for a job search. I returned for my first appointment with Quest at the end of August; a woman named Lana was my career counselor, and she told me that it would cost me $3,000 if I decided to let them find me a job. After our meeting, I prayed silently and long for guidance. I didn't know what to do, but I decided to take a risk, not knowing if I had made the right choice. I worked on the Quest profile that was supposed to define what job I was interested in and drove back and forth to Atlanta for meetings with my counselor. I had my first appointment with Quest in early September and met other clients involved in the job search.

During the month of October, I was stressed out, since I was due to retire on the thirty-first (Halloween day). I started house hunting in Atlanta, checked out some places in northwest Atlanta, and finally found a small house in Smyrna to rent. I spent mid-October out processing and was having problems with Quest in preparing my resume. I only had a few weeks to retire, and they didn't have this done yet. I made arrangements to have my household goods packed and moved to my new house by the end of October.

Mr. Lynch and the students gave me a going-away party, and four of my favorite students from Saudi Arabia took Chantay and me out to dinner and spent big bucks on us. Chantay would leave in November to go to Fort Polk for two months and then relocate to New Jersey to work in her new job's home office.

Well, my year in the pit with Mr. Lynch was almost over, and I was ready to become a civilian. I ended this job feeling triumphant and received my final military OER. Mr. Lynch stated: "*Major Byrd demonstrated exceptional managerial abilities while working in a highly sensitive area in support of the U.S. Army Signal Corps Security Assistance Mission. She is a strongly motivated person who aggressively looks for ways to improve operations with only minimal guidance. She exercises strong supervision of subordinates and willingly accepts responsibility. She completely revised the command briefing for international students to include thirty-five-millimeter slides and narratives for foreign visitors to Fort Gordon. She also developed an administration/operations SOP that standardized procedures defining job descriptions and responsible staff elements. For her outstanding effort in the renovation of the student barracks, we presented her with the TRADOC installation of excellence award. Working in an area requiring tact and diplomacy, Major Byrd has consistently achieved the best possible atmosphere of international cooperation with military students from around the world. Her professionalism and sound judgment attests to her total dedication to the U.S. Army."*

My rating from my intermediate rater, the LTC, stated: *"Major Byrd is an outstanding officer with the uncanny ability to make things happen and get the job done. She provided the necessary military interface in the unit which facilitated the execution of several significant initiatives. Her efforts with the officer-student sponsorship and officer-course briefing programs significantly enhanced the integration of international officers into both the Signal Officer Basic and Advanced programs. She was solely responsible for the barracks upgrade programs, which turned the International Training Barracks into a model facility. Her can do attitude enhanced the effectiveness of the unit, the Signal Brigade, and Fort Gordon."*

I also received a rating from the senior rater, a colonel, saying *"Major Byrd did an outstanding job working with a multitude of foreign officers and noncommissioned officers sent here for training from countries located all over the world. I am particularly impressed with her exceptional efforts in getting the allied student barracks complex upgraded to its present high level of excellence. She exhibits good staff skills, which make her a success in army-military police or personnel-related staff assignment. If recalled to active duty during future mobilization, I recommend she be sent to Fort McClellan or any other TRADOC school to work in training related to job as a major or LTC."*

I was presented a Meritorious Service Award upon my departure, which read in part *"Major Byrd distinguished herself by exceptional meritorious service as the deputy international training officer. She demonstrated initiative, enthusiasm, and keen foresight in the performance of duties in an extremely sensitive duty position assisting more than four hundred international military students from approximately sixty different nations as they undertook highly technical courses of instruction at the U.S. Army Signal School. Her leadership, diplomacy, dedicated service, and superb organizational ability contributed immeasurably to the accomplishment of the unit mission. She has consistently been a loyal and determined member of the organization, often using her own free time to assist foreign students with whatever problems they may have, regardless of how critical or how sensitive the situation would appear. Her outstanding skill, self-reliance, and cheerful, cooperative attitude coupled with her superior organizational ability has earned her the respect and admiration of both superiors and subordinates. Major Byrd's action and accomplishments far exceeded normal expectations and reflect great credit upon herself, the division, the brigade, and the U.S. Army."*

I opted not to participate in a retirement ceremony (parade and pinning on medal), but instead quietly said my good-byes to all, out processed, and headed to Atlanta. I received a letter from the two-star post commander stating *"This nation is grateful for your dedication, loyalty, and faithfulness during your many years of military service. The accomplishments of soldiers such as yourself have contributed immeasurably to our country in war and in peace. Although retiring from active duty, you will always be part of the military family. The people of this nation wish you continued success in the years ahead and extend their thanks for your service to your country and the U.S. Army."*

Somewhere in my military papers, I have a certificate of retirement that I received later, signed by President George Bush Sr. *Whippee do-do.* My military business was finished—a goal accomplished with twenty-one years of adventurous, yet exasperating valley experiences—growing, learning, defeating, and triumphant military service behind me. *It's all over, Lee—unfinished business,* fini*!*

I completed my out processing, received my blue retirement ID, and picked up my travel money from finance. My retirement came on Halloween day, and it took me thirty minutes to finalize all paperwork. I felt good about my unfinished business. My spiritual military journey was completed; I had no regrets, and I departed Fort Gordon with no desire to see anyone as I drove off the installation heading to Atlanta.

It was time to decide which fork to take in the road that faces me now. Would my decision be the right one? Are more valleys awaiting me? Have I finally arrived at my destination, or would the mysterious journey continue? Now the camera is rolling for the real life adventure awaiting me in my new quest in the civilian Promised Land. The saga will continue in my second book, which will include the adventures, trials, and tribulations I faced after retiring from the army.

Thank you for traveling with me through my military-struggling-but-victorious spiritual journey as a *black woman in the white man's army.* God bless you all. **Everything I experience is part of the divine order to help me discover who I am!**

EPILOGUE

At age forty-eight, I retired from the U.S. Army and thanked God for the twenty years, ten months, and seventeen days of a successful career and for helping me survive the numerous obstacles that crossed my path. As my spiritual military journey came to a quiet ending, I prayed and hoped that I had done well in God's eyesight. I tried to be *all that I could be* and did the best I could under conditions that I had no control over. I learned many worthwhile lessons through all my various and sundry experiences, tried to do unto others as I would have them do unto me; and at the end of my journey, I surrendered myself to God.

As I read and included my OERs in this book, the meaning of my past military life was more defined. This is why I included these excerpts for the reader to peruse—I did each job to the highest standards possible despite the obstacles. These evaluations told the real story about my service to my country and, in turn, gave me positive feedback on my overall performance of duty and the virtues I actually possess. However, the *written words* in my OERs were meaningless throughout my career, because no one at the higher level (white men) were willing to *punch my ticket* in upward mobility. Instead, I was often the punching bag. Even though I did not receive the appropriate rank I rightfully deserved, deep inside I know that my potential was and still is unlimited. So be it.

I don't know if I touched many lives during my past military journey, but I do hope that the *real me* was evident to those who interacted with me. I did not receive all the awards and ribbons that I rightfully earned, but as I have stated previously: "my rewards and praise are not to be of this earth. My payoff will be decided by the supreme commander in chief, who is not a white man wearing a green uniform."

I often wondered *what if* things would have been different in my choices and military assignments; however, I'll never know because the past is gone, never to be again. As I pondered on my past military quest, a spiritual voice within spoke to me: "You are no longer in charge of your destiny. You need to cease trying to take control and make life happen for you. When God comes to you and you let him take control, you will experience a resurrection to a new level of living. He will provide you with a new set of desires, a new purpose, and a new perspective. Your talents and opportunities are nothing but a gift from God, and you must use them for his glory. God will show you the way and define your duty and mission daily.

"Even if you have faith as small as a mustard seed, you can say to this mountain, move from here to there, and it will move. Nothing will be impossible for you. God is growing a mustard tree out of you. He will grow something substantial and useful out of the tiny seeds of what you are today."

As my personal awareness and spiritual growth enhanced, I found myself at the fork of another road, awaiting the tasking that may or may not lead me to the mountaintop. Whatever God has planned for me, I am ready. My military business is finished, and it is time for a new beginning as a civilian. I am indeed blessed, and I give thanks to God for the manifestation of my goodness. "Thank you, dear Father."

An awareness of spirit will manifest itself in ways that meet my every need.